MULTIPLAN™
MADE EASY

MULTIPLAN™ MADE EASY

Walter A. Ettlin

Osborne **McGraw-Hill**
Berkeley, California

Published by
Osborne **McGraw-Hill**
2600 Tenth Street
Berkeley, California 94710
U.S.A.

For information on translations and book
distributors outside of the U.S.A., please write to
Osborne **McGraw-Hill** at the above address.

Multiplan is a trademark of Microsoft Corporation.
Multiplan™ *Made Easy* is not sponsored or approved by
or connected with Microsoft Corporation. All references
to Multiplan in the text of this book are to the trademark
of Microsoft Corporation.

MULTIPLAN™ MADE EASY

34567890 DODO 898765

ISBN 0-07-881135-x

Cynthia Hudson, Acquisitions Editor
Kevin Gleason, Technical Editor
Joseph E. Thier of Applied Computer Consulting (Oakland, CA),
    Technical Reviewer
Fran Haselsteiner, Copy Editor
Richard Cash, Book Design
Yashi Okita, Cover Design

TABLE OF CONTENTS

About the Author

Walter A. Ettlin has instructed California high school students for 22 years. He has taught math, physics, and computer programming, as well as word processing and spreadsheet applications. Ettlin formerly was on the Board of Directors of CUE (Computer-Using Educators) and is co-owner of EAS (Educators' Administrative Software), which provides administrative software to schools. Walter is the author of our *WordStar® Made Easy book and co-author of The MBASIC® Handbook.*

Acknowledgments

My sincere thanks to my wife Cynthia, who worked long hours as she typed and retyped the many drafts of the manuscript; to my son Eric, whose artistic impressions lightened these pages; to Mary Borchers, whose editorial expertise contributed greatly to the final tone of this book.

W.E.

Introduction

Multiplan Made Easy is a series of tutorials that can help you take full advantage of the electronic spreadsheet program, Multiplan. This book will enable you to design and create your own worksheets.

From its introduction in 1979 to the present, the electronic spreadsheet for microcomputers has grown greatly in capability. Multiplan, a second-generation spreadsheet, has many powerful features that did not exist in the original programs, including:

1. A large worksheet area—63 columns by 255 rows.
2. Multiple windows that allow you to view up to eight sections of the worksheet on the screen at one time.
3. The ability to link the active worksheet with worksheets contained on diskettes or a hard disk.
4. Variable column widths.
5. A continuous format that allows you to enter lengthy data in one cell and display it in the next cell or cells.
6. Automatic recalculation.
7. The ability to sort, or rearrange, both text and numbers.
8. The ability to protect cells from accidental change or erasure by locking their contents.

As a financial spreadsheet, Multiplan can take the drudgery out of bookkeeping tasks, from a family budget to the budget of a small company. If you enter new data, you need not recalculate the entire worksheet: Multiplan does this for you. The changes are automatic (unless you choose to control them), and the results can be seen almost immediately.

Multiplan is not used only with financial records. For example, in education it can be used to maintain students' scholastic records, to analyze tests, and to print out grades. Its built-in functions make it very useful in technical applications as well: for example, in engineering, for solving stress problems; in architecture, for calculating costs of materials; and in navigation, for determining positions.

Getting the Most From This Book

This book is a series of tutorials to help you take full advantage of Multiplan in designing and creating your own worksheets. It is intended to be used while you are working with Multiplan at a computer. As you are introduced to each command or function, you are given simple examples to enter so you can see the results immediately. In addition, screen displays on the page enable you to check your results. After each example, you then use the new commands in combination with those previously learned in larger and more practical worksheets.

At the end of each chapter, simple exercises reinforce processes and concepts. These exercises are an important part of becoming proficient in Multiplan, to which the old adage, "You learn by doing," certainly applies.

The first ten chapters cover most of Multiplan's commands as well as some functions that greatly simplify and speed up the building of worksheets. The last four chapters cover the remaining functions and the iteration process, a tool that contributes greatly to Multiplan's power as an electronic spreadsheet.

Types of Computers

Multiplan runs on many different computers and under several operating systems, including PC DOS, MS DOS, CP/M, and CP/M-86. If your computer uses one of these operating systems, you should have virtually no trouble implementing Multiplan.

There are various versions of Multiplan available for these systems, but all contain the same commands and functions. The biggest change in the latest IBM version — version 1.1 — is that it can be placed on the IBM PC XT's hard disk and can support the directory system of that disk. Other changes in this version include

1. Allowing it to take advantage of up to 512K (kilobytes) of the computer's memory.
2. Increased precision for the math transcendental functions (such as SIN, COS, and EXP).
3. Increasing the print width capability to 512 characters.
4. An updated manual.

The tutorials in this book use the IBM implementation of Multiplan 1.1 on the PC. If your computer's keyboard is different from the PC keyboard (shown later in this Introduction), if it does not have function keys, if the function keys are not supported by Multiplan, or if it has no arrow keys for moving the cell pointer, you will find Appendix A useful. It tells you which keys to use on your keyboard.

Care of Disks

Floppy disks can last for years, but they can also be destroyed in a fraction of a second. Because the loss of a file or a complete disk can be so inconvenient, take these precautions to get the maximum life from your disks:

ALWAYS:
1. Use felt-tip pens when labeling a disk.
2. Hold the disk by the corners.
3. When not in use, keep the disks in their protective envelopes and in an appropriate holder.

NEVER:
1. Write with pencil or ballpoint pen on the disk.
2. Touch the exposed portion of the disk.
3. Expose disks to direct sunlight.
4. Allow magnets near disks.
5. Attach papers to a disk with paper clips.
6. Clean the disk surface with any liquids.

Figure I-1 shows 5 1/4- and 8-inch disks. Both disks have what is called a *write-protect notch,* which enables you to protect the disk from accidental writing or alteration of its contents. The two notches work in opposite ways, however. To write-protect a 5 1/4-inch disk, you *cover* the write-protect notch. To write-protect an 8-inch disk, you *uncover* the notch. If you use 5 1/4-inch disks, it is a good idea to write-protect your Multiplan backup disk by covering this notch with a write-protect tab. Tabs are included when you purchase disks.

Getting Started With Multiplan

Once Multiplan is loaded, it operates virtually the same on all computers (the Macintosh is the only exception). But because there are different sources and versions of Multiplan, how you set it up on your disk may vary slightly from the description here, which is for IBM Multiplan version 1.1 using PC DOS 2.0. Regardless of what version of Multiplan you have, you should always work with a backup copy and keep the original in a safe place. Consult your Multiplan manual for the proper procedure for making a backup copy on your system.

The IBM version of Multiplan 1.1 for PC DOS allows you to make only one copy of the program, so it is important that you protect it from possible damage. Make your one and only copy by carefully following the directions on pages 0-31 to 0-40 of the IBM Multiplan manual. Put your original disk away for safekeeping, and immediately place a write-protect tab on your backup disk. You will use the backup disk only to load Multiplan, never to save worksheets. This practice will minimize wear on the disk, and write-protecting it makes it impossible to erase the Multiplan program accidentally.

Prepare a disk for storing the worksheets you will create. The files you need on this disk depend on the amount of memory in your computer. If there is less than 128K, you need two files, MP.SYS and MP.HLP. If your computer has 128K or more, MP.SYS is loaded in the computer along with Multiplan, and you need only add the file MP.HLP to your data disk. Now proceed to format a disk and copy the required file or files. This is the disk you will use to save the worksheets

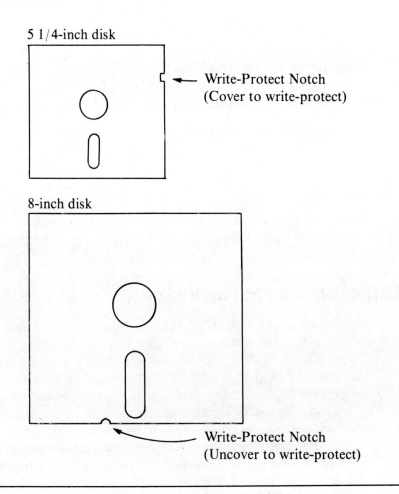

5 1/4-inch disk

Write-Protect Notch
(Cover to write-protect)

8-inch disk

Write-Protect Notch
(Uncover to write-protect)

Figure I-1. *The two most common sizes of floppy disks*

you develop as you work with this book. Any subsequent disks you prepare for storing worksheets should contain the same files.

Loading Multiplan

The way you load Multiplan depends on the version you have as well as your computer configuration (such as whether you have one disk drive, two drives, or a hard disk). The following method is suggested for an IBM PC system with two disk drives using DOS 2.0 and IBM Multiplan version 1.1 for PC DOS.

The IBM version 1.1 of Multiplan for PC DOS 2.0 does not "boot up" your machine; that is, it does not contain the operating system needed to get your computer running. So you put your PC DOS 2.0 system disk in drive A and boot your computer in the normal manner. Leave the system disk in drive A, and place the backup copy of Multiplan in drive B. Type **MP80** and press ENTER. (If you are using an MS DOS or a CP/M version of Multiplan, you just type **MP** and press ENTER.) When Multiplan is loaded and the red operating light of the drive is turned off, remove the Multiplan disk and store it properly. Now place the data disk in the drive and you are ready to save the worksheets you create. In Chapter 2 you will see how to save a worksheet.

Naming Files

The term *file* applies to any information saved on either a floppy or a hard disk; a file may be something as simple as your first worksheet or as complicated as the Multiplan program itself. As you work through this book, you will save some of the worksheets in files for later use. In these cases you will be given suggested filenames, but you will also need to create filenames for your own worksheets. There are a few rules for assigning a name to a file, but fortunately, they are the same for both CP/M and MS DOS or PC DOS.

1. A filename can contain up to eight characters.
2. The first character in the name must be a letter and then may be followed by any of these characters:

   A-Z 0-9 $ & # @ ! % ` ( ) − { } _ ^~

3. The name can be (though it need not be) followed by a period and what is called an *extension*, three additional characters. The extension is commonly used to distinguish different types of files. For example, .MP might refer to Multiplan files and .WS to WordStar files.

Examples of valid filenames are

CH14.WAE
INTEREST.MP
WINDOW.MP
FIG#3.WS
HELLO

The last example is a reminder that the extension is not required. Normally the name you use will give you some kind of a clue to the contents of the file.

The Keyboard

Multiplan runs on different computers; thus, it must work on a variety of terminals and keyboards. Here the IBM PC keyboard and those of its look-alikes will be described. If you are using a keyboard that does not have all of these keys, refer to appendix A to find the generic codes that you can use on your keyboard to get the same results.

Most of the keys on the keyboard automatically repeat when held down — a great convenience when you are editing or when you want to move the cell pointer rapidly.

The IBM PC keyboard is divided into three sections, as shown in Figure I-2. Let's consider each section individually.

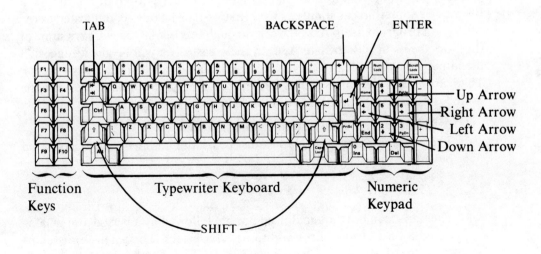

Figure I-2. *The IBM PC keyboard*

Function Keys

When pressed, each of the function keys, FI to FI0, sends Multiplan a specific command. These are the most frequently used commands in Multiplan, and each will be described as its use is required in the worksheets developed in this book. Appendix A gives a summary of their uses, along with the keys to substitute if your keyboard does not have function keys.

Typewriter Keyboard

This section of the keyboard is fairly standard for all computers, although three keys on the IBM PC have symbols that designate specific operations. Throughout this book you will see the standard terms rather than the symbols, so you should familiarize yourself with them:

IBM Symbol	Standard Term
←	BACKSPACE
↵	ENTER
⇄	TAB
⇧	SHIFT

Numeric Keypad

The numeric keypad on the right side of the keyboard serves two functions. When Multiplan is loaded, this keypad is set to move the cell pointer and scroll the worksheet. For these operations you use all of the numbered keys 1-9 except 5. But if you wish, you can change the mode of entering numbers by pressing the NUMLOCK key. In this case, pressing a number key on the numeric keypad enters a number rather than moving the cell pointer. To change back to original mode, press the NUMLOCK key again. It is a "toggle," changing back and forth from one mode to the other.

Whether you use the numeric keypad to enter numbers or move the cell pointer is a matter of personal preference; but you will probably find it more convenient to leave this keypad in its original mode and use the number keys along the top of the typewriter section for numeric entry. Again, if your terminal does not have arrow keys to move the cell pointer, Appendix A lists the keys that will do this.

The Multiplan
Worksheet

Place your start-up disk in drive A and your Multiplan disk in drive B. Turn on the computer. When the A> prompt appears, type **B:** and press ENTER. You have just logged onto drive B; the prompt B> now appears. Type **MP80** to load the Multiplan program. The IBM logo and copyright notices are briefly displayed, and you are presented with the Multiplan *worksheet,* shown in Figure 1-1. Several key features of the Multiplan worksheet appear in this initial display. Each is identified in Figure 1-1.

Window

The window number, shown in the upper-left corner of the screen, refers to the *active window* area of a worksheet. In the initial display the window number is 1. A Multiplan worksheet can have up to eight active windows. You'll work with this feature in Chapter 8, when more than one active window will be on the screen at a time.

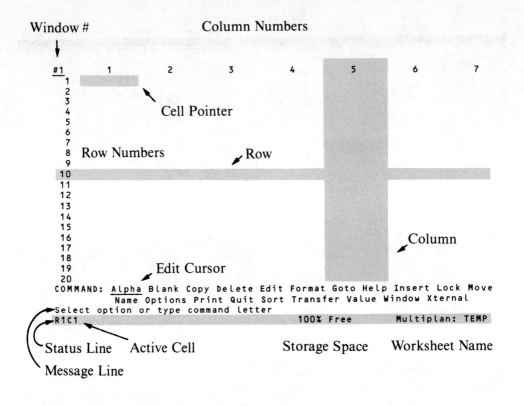

Figure 1-1.   *The Multiplan worksheet*

Rows and Columns

The numbers across the top of the screen indicate the worksheet *columns*, which extend from top to bottom. The numbers at the left of the screen indicate the *rows*, which extend across the screen. On the initial screen there are 7 columns, numbered 1 through 7, and 20 rows, numbered 1 through 20.

Your screen displays only a portion of the Multiplan worksheet at any one time. The full worksheet is a grid constructed of 63 columns and 255 rows, as Figure 1-2 suggests. As you will see later, the screen display can be moved to show any portion of the worksheet.

The Active Cell and Cell Pointer

The bright rectangle in the upper-left corner of the screen, row 1, column 1, is the *cell pointer.* The cell pointer indicates the *active cell,* the row-by-column area where data is entered into the worksheet. Each cell is identified by its coordinates—for example, R1C1 for row 1, column 1. Before you begin entering data, you need to see how the cell pointer is moved about the worksheet.

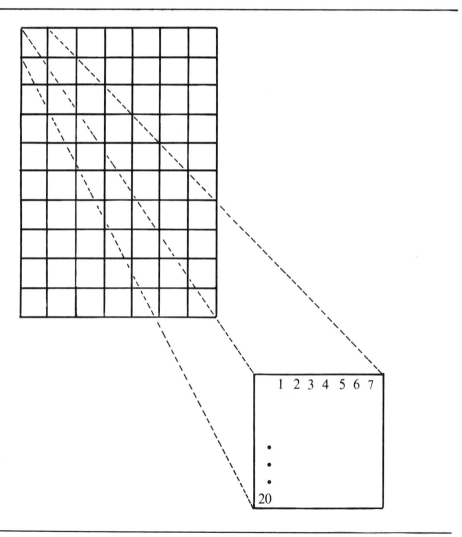

Figure 1-2.   *The screen displays only a small portion of the total worksheet*

Moving the Cell Pointer

The numeric keypad on the right side of the keyboard has four arrow keys. Pressing any one of these will move the cell pointer in the direction of the arrow — left, right, up, or down. Practice moving the active cell around the screen by using the keys.

Now return the cell pointer to the first row and press the up arrow key. You will hear a beep. This is Multiplan's way of saying that it cannot comply with your command (in this case, you cannot move the pointer up any farther because the first row is the topmost row).

As you use the arrow keys, you may encounter their *automatic repeat* feature. If you hold a key down for more than a second, the cell pointer will rapidly move from column to column or row to row in the direction of the arrow. Try this feature to see how it works.

Now, with the cell pointer at any position on the screen, press the HOME key (key 7 on the numeric keypad). The pointer will immediately move to the upper-left corner of the screen. This corner is called the *home* position, and pressing the HOME key will always move the pointer there.

The Command Line and Edit Cursor

The *command line* appears on the third and fourth lines from the bottom of the screen. It lists all of Multiplan's primary commands. The bright rectangle over the Alpha command is called the *edit cursor*. To move the edit cursor from one command to another, use the space bar or the BACKSPACE key. The space bar moves the cursor to the right; the BACKSPACE key moves it to the left. Try these keys a few times to move the cursor over different commands in the command line.

A command may be selected in either of two ways. You can move the edit cursor to the command and then press ENTER; or you can type the first letter of the command—for example, pressing **E** will select the Edit command. (Throughout this book, instead of being told to press, say, **E** for Edit, you will be told to press **Edit**. You press only the **boldface** letter.) Try selecting a few commands by both methods; after you have selected a command, press the ESC key to return to the command line. You will learn how to use individual commands starting in Chapter 2.

The Message Line

The *message line* appears at the bottom of your screen. It contains a brief instruction, sometimes called a *prompt,* of what to enter for the command you have selected. Initially, before you have selected any commands, the message line reads

Select option or type command letter

Now, with the edit cursor on Alpha, press ENTER. The message line now reads

Enter text (no double quotes)

Press the ESC key to return to the command line. A message often appears on the message line to prompt the correct use of the selected command.

The Status Line

The bottom line on the screen, the *status line,* contains three items of information: the position of the active cell, the percentage of free memory, and the filename of your worksheet.

At the beginning of the status line, the position of the active cell is given by row and column numbers, for example, R1C1. This notation is used throughout this book to identify particular cell locations on the worksheet. Using the arrow keys, move the cell pointer around the screen and notice how the identity of the current active cell changes.

The amount of free memory, given as a percentage, refers to the amount of space left free in your computer's memory for storage of data. Of course, when Multiplan first comes up all the memory is available and the screen indicates "100% Free." This percent will change as you enter data into your Multiplan worksheet. (The percentage displayed on your screen may, on occasion, not match those indicated in this book, since your computer may have a different amount of memory.)

The right end of the status line shows the name of the worksheet you are working with. On the initial Multiplan screen, the name TEMP is assigned. When you have entered data into the worksheet and are ready to save it, you'll have the option of changing the name to whatever you prefer.

In Chapter 2 you'll see that the status line contains a fourth item, the contents of the active cell.

Finally, a fifth item can appear on the status line. In the space between the words "Free" and "Multiplan," the letters NL will appear if you press the NUM LOCK (numeric lock) key. These letters indicate that the numeric keypad is in numeric mode: pressing the keys will enter numbers into the worksheet, rather than move the cell pointer or scroll the screen (discussed shortly). Pressing the NUM LOCK key a second time will eliminate the letters NL and disable numeric lock, returning you to the original mode of the numeric keypad.

A second set of letters can appear in this space: the letters SL, which appear when the SCROLL LOCK key is pressed. You'll experiment with this feature shortly. Again, pressing the SCROLL LOCK key a second time will eliminate the letters from the status line.

Scrolling Through the Worksheet

When the cell pointer reaches the right edge of the screen it can no longer move right; instead, the worksheet moves left a column at a time. To see this, use the arrow keys to move the cell pointer to R1C7 (row 1, column 7) and press the right arrow key once more. All the columns shift to the left; the farthest right column is now number 8, and the first column on the left is now number 2. Press again and the farthest right column becomes number 9 and the farthest left number becomes 3. To return the screen to its initial display, press the HOME key and then press the left arrow key twice. Your screen will appear as it did initially.

You can do the same with the down arrow key: move the cursor to row 20; then press it again. Rows 2 through 210 are now displayed.

Moving the cell pointer so that the worksheet shifts — that is, changing the rows or columns displayed on the screen — is called *scrolling*. You *scroll down* to view higher-numbered rows, *scroll up* to view lower-numbered rows, *scroll right* to view higher-numbered columns, and *scroll left* to view lower-numbered columns.

Now let's examine what happens when the SCROLL LOCK key is pressed. With the screen displaying columns 1 through 7 and rows 1 through 20, move the cell pointer to R10C4 and press SCROLL LOCK. The letters SL appear on the status line. Press the right arrow key. What happens? It appears that the cell pointer moves to the left. But examine the column numbers across the top of the screen: the column numbers 2 through 8 are displayed. Notice also that the cell pointer is still in R10C4.

Remember that the Multiplan worksheet is 63 columns by 255 rows. The screen has moved over the worksheet, displaying a new column to the right, column 8. The cell pointer will stay in R10C4 unless it comes in contact with the top or left edge of the screen; in that case, the cell pointer will move so that it remains on the portion of the worksheet displayed on the screen. Experiment with this scroll lock feature using all four arrow keys. You will find it very useful later on when developing worksheets containing more than a screenful of data.

A Faster Way to Scroll

Besides scrolling a row or column at a time with the arrow keys, you may scroll a *page* at a time. Think of a page as the portion of the worksheet you see on the screen at any one time — say rows 1-20 and columns 1-7. Figure 1-3 is a partial diagram of the overall worksheet divided into pages. To try scrolling by pages, press the PGDN (page down) key. The display changes to an entirely new page, and the screen moves down 20 rows, displaying numbers 21 through 40. Similarly, the PGUP (page up) key moves the screen *up* 20 rows. Press the PGUP key now, and you'll return to rows 1 through 20.

There are no "page left" or "page right" keys, but you can move the screen a full page (seven columns) left or right by simultaneously pressing the CTRL key and the left or right arrow key. For example, press the CTRL and right arrow keys to move the screen one page to the right; the column numbers displayed at the top of the screen are now 8 through 14. Now press the CTRL and left arrow keys to move the screen one page to the left.

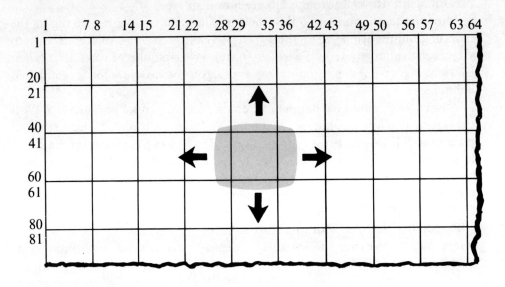

Figure 1-3.   *Partial view of worksheet divided into pages*

Moving the Cell Pointer Long Distances: GOTO

Another way to move the cell pointer long distances on the display screen or on the worksheet is to use the Goto command. Let's try this now.

1. With the cell pointer still in R5C5, press **G**oto; your GOTO command line displays the following subcommand options:

   GOTO: <u>Name</u> Row-col Window

2. Press **R** to choose the Row-col subcommand and the command line displays

   GOTO row: 5 column:5

3. In the "row:" field type **50**.
4. Press the TAB key to move to the next field.
5. In the "column:" field type **45** and press ENTER.

Your active cell pointer moves to R50C45.

Goto is an easy way to move large distances on the screen or worksheet because it will take you immediately to any cell. For short distances, the arrow keys are an easier way to move about the screen.

Use the GOTO/Row-col command to return to the beginning of the worksheet, R1C1. The other Goto subcommands, Name and Window, are discussed in Chapters 8 and 10.

You should now be familiar with the layout of the Multiplan worksheet and its elements. You may move on to Chapter 2 to begin entering data in your worksheet, or reset your computer (return to DOS) by pressing the CTRL, ALT, and DEL keys simultaneously.

Exercises

1. Practice using the keys that move the cell pointer about the screen. Do this with both the arrow keys and the keys that move the worksheet a full page at a time.

2. If you are using a computer other than the IBM, and the keys that move the cell pointer are not designated on the keyboard, indicate the keys to press for cursor movement and scrolling on a 3-by-5-inch reference card. (The CTRL key is represented by ^.)

Cell Pointer

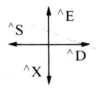

Scrolling by the Page

Entering Data

Commands

- Alpha
- Value
- FORMAT WIDTH
- FORMAT cells
- TRANSFER SAVE
- QUIT

Now that you have been introduced to the key features of the Multiplan worksheet and have had some practice in moving the cell pointer about the screen, you can begin entering data.

Figure 2-1 shows the baseball standings for the Western Division of the National League. You will use this data to develop your first worksheet.

Escape From Trouble

Before you begin, a note of caution: If at any time while entering data you should accidentally press a wrong key and an unintended command is displayed on the command line, press the ESC key; Multiplan will return the full command menu to the command line.

```
                              NATIONAL LEAGUE
                               WEST DIVISION

                         W         L        Pct.       GB
        Los Angeles      81        59       0.579      0.0
        Atlanta          79        61       0.564      2.0
        Houston          73        66       0.525      7.5
        San Diego        70        72       0.493     12.0
        San Francisco    67        74       0.475     14.5
        Cincinnati       64        78       0.451     18.0
```

Figure 2-1.   *The table you are going to build*

Entering Names and Numbers

Enter the team names first. Move the cell pointer to R5C1 (row 5, column 1), where you will enter the first team name.

Alpha

Since team names are made up only of letters, or alphabetic characters, you use the *Alpha* (short for "alphabetic") command to enter this data.

With the edit cursor over the Alpha command, press ENTER. The command line now contains only the word "ALPHA:" followed by the cursor waiting for you to enter the alphabetic data. The message line reads

Enter text (no double quotes)

Type the first team name, **Los Angeles**. Your command line now reads

ALPHA: Los Angeles

Now that you have completed the entry and are ready to start another, tell Multiplan by pressing ENTER. The date you typed, Los Angeles, is transferred to the active cell. Don't worry for now that the last S is missing; you'll take care of that detail shortly. Note that the status line shows a copy of the data entered in the active cell.

Press the down arrow key to move the cell pointer to R6C1. Again press ENTER to select the Alpha command, which the edit cursor is highlighting, and type the name **Atlanta**. This time, instead of pressing ENTER to conclude your entry, press the down arrow key. The text, Atlanta, is transferred to the active cell, just as if you had pressed ENTER; but the cell pointer has moved to the cell below, making it the new active cell. The command line shows a new command,

ALPHA/VALUE:

The word "Alpha" stands not only for "alphabetic" but also for "alpha-numeric," which refers to data consisting of letters and numbers. Numbers in alphanumeric entries are treated just like letters of the alphabet; that is, no mathematical operations can be performed on them, and they cannot be entered in formulas. For instance, if you enter **1/5** using the Alpha command, you will see 1/5 printed on the worksheet; but if you enter **1/5** using the Value command, you will see 0.2, the quotient of 1/5, printed on the worksheet.

An alphanumeric entry is also called a *text* entry, an entry in which each character is printed exactly as you typed or entered it. To make a text entry, you must use the Alpha command. But how does the ALPHA/VALUE command allow you to distinguish between entries of *text* and *numeric data?* Simple: if you have ALPHA/VALUE on the command line and the first character you type is a letter, Multiplan will treat your entry as text (and the command line will display "ALPHA:"). But if the first character you type is any digit, 0-9; the mathematical operators +, −, or =; the left parenthesis, (; or double quotation marks, ", Multiplan will treat your entry as numeric data (and the command line will display "VALUE:"). If any of these characters (except the equals sign) is used to select the Value command, it becomes the first character of your cell entry. You may find it convenient to select the Value command by pressing = when non-numeric data is to be entered.

Now back to constructing the table of baseball standings. With the command line reading ALPHA/VALUE, type the name of the next team, **Houston**. Since it starts with an H, Multiplan automatically selects the Alpha command. Complete the entry by pressing the down arrow key, and use the same procedure to type in the remaining team names.

Value

After you've typed in the last team name, Cincinnati, use the right arrow and up arrow keys to move the cell pointer to R5C2. Ignore the column headings for now and begin entering the number of wins per team in column 2. The command line prompt still reads "ALPHA/VALUE:". You want to type **81**. When you press the 8 key, the command line changes to "VALUE:". Use the down arrow key to complete each entry in the column.

When you have finished column 2, begin typing columns 3, 4, and 5, inserting the games lost, percentage of wins, and games behind for each team.

Your screen should now look like Figure 2-2. To make it more like the original table, you will need to make modifications.

Changing Column Width

The longest names in the table, Los Angeles and San Francisco, have been *truncated* (shortened) to just ten letters. This is because Multiplan columns are ten characters in width unless you change them. The values that Multiplan automatically supplies for a command — in this case, ten for column width — are called *default* values. You will see how to change various default command values as the need arises. The following section explains how to change the width of a column with the Format command.

Format

A width of 13 characters is needed in column 1 to fully display the longest team name, San Francisco. Begin by moving the cell pointer to column 1 (the easiest way is to press the HOME key, which will move the cell pointer to R1C1). For the Format command to be selected, the command menu, the full list of command options, must be displayed on the command line. If the command menu is not displayed, press the ESC key. Then press Format.

The Format command line displays four subcommands:

FORMAT: <u>Cells</u> Default Options Width

```
                 1           2           3           4           5
    1
    2
    3
    4
    5  Los Angele     81          59         0.579        0
    6  Atlanta        79          61         0.564        2
    7  Houston        73          66         0.525        7.5
    8  San Diego      70          72         0.493        12
    9  San Franci     67          74         0.475        14.5
   10  Cincinnati     64          78         0.451        18
```

Figure 2-2. *The results of using the Alpha and ALPHA/VALUE commands*

You select any of the four subcommands just as you've selected the main commands: simply press the first letter of the subcommand, or move the edit cursor with the space bar or BACKSPACE key to highlight your selection and then press ENTER. In this case, press **Width**.

Format/Width

Selecting the FORMAT WIDTH command presents you with new command and message lines:

                                        Field 1   *Field 2*   *Field 3*

FORMAT WIDTH in chars or d(efault): $\underset{\sim}{\text{d}}$ column: $\underset{\sim}{1}$ through: $\underset{\sim}{1}$
Enter a number, or d for default

Notice that on the command line there are three *fields*, or areas in which you can type an entry, each distinguished by a colon. All three fields affect how the FORMAT WIDTH command changes your worksheet. The first field is for the desired column *width* measured in characters, the second field is for a *beginning column* number, and the third field is for an *ending column* number. In each field Multiplan automatically enters a value, the default value: in field 1, column width *d* (for "default," in this case, ten characters); and in fields 2 and 3, the number of the column that the cell pointer is in. You can change the values in the three fields.

To move the edit cursor from one field to the next, press the TAB key. If you are in the third field and press the TAB key, the edit cursor moves back to the first field. Try this a few times to see how the cursor moves. Notice also how the message line changes when you move from field 1 to field 2 and back from field 3 to field 1.

Column 1 must be at least 13 characters wide, but allow a couple of extra spaces to make it 15 characters wide. With the edit cursor in the first field, type **15**. Since you're only widening column 1, the default values in fields 1 and 2 are correct; so you can simply press ENTER to carry out, or *execute,* the FORMAT WIDTH command. But instead, let's practice correcting typing errors. Press the TAB key to move the cursor to field 2. Although 1 is the correct value for the beginning column number, type in another number. To erase it, press the BACKSPACE key and type in **1**. Press the TAB key, type another number over the correct default value, press the BACKSPACE key, and type in **1**.

Finally, to execute the FORMAT WIDTH command, press ENTER. Column 1 is now 15 characters wide on your worksheet, and all the letters in the names

Los Angeles and San Francisco are displayed. (Although the complete names did not appear on the screen previously, they were held in the computer's memory.)

Now move the cell pointer to R4C2, press ENTER to select the Alpha command, and type the column headings (**W** for wins, **L** for losses, **Pct.** for percentage, and **GB** for games behind) in the appropriate columns (see Figure 2-1). You have now entered all the data and headings. Unfortunately, the alignment within the columns is not satisfactory.

First use the Format command again to change the widths of columns 2 and 3 so your worksheet more closely resembles the format of the original table (Figure 2-1). Make each column six characters wide. Move the cell pointer to column 2 and press **F**ormat and then **W**idth. Now type **6** for the width, press the TAB key twice to move the edit cursor to the third field, and type a **3** there. The FORMAT WIDTH command line should look like this:

FORMAT WIDTH in chars or d(efault): 6   column: 2   through: 3

Press ENTER and notice how the screen changes immediately to conform to the new column width.

To finish adjusting the column widths, change the width of column 5 to six characters, using the same procedure as before. Column 4 can remain at the default width of ten characters.

Centering Data

The columns are now the proper width, but the column headings need to be aligned within the columns. Two of Multiplan's defaults make this necessary. Multiplan *left-justifies* text entries; that is, it aligns data at the left of a column. Multiplan also *right-justifies* numeric data; it aligns data at the right of the column. As the following example shows, this is why the headings are aligned differently from the numeric data within columns.

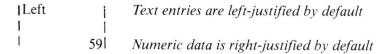

The Format command can be used to change the justification of either numeric or text entries, like the headings in a table.

Format/Cells

Move the cell pointer to R4C2, over the W. Press Format; the edit cursor is over the Cells subcommand, so press ENTER. The command and message lines appear as follows:

FORMAT cells: <u>R4C2</u>   alignment:(Def)Ctr Gen Left Right −
       format code:(Def)Cont Exp Fix Gen Int $ * % − # of decimals: 0
Enter reference to cell or group of cells

The FORMAT cells command line has four fields. Use the TAB key to move the edit cursor to each of these fields and notice how the message line changes. The "alignment:" field and the "format code:" field both have several options. The option that is active is identified by the parentheses enclosing it. Currently the Def (default) option is active for both fields.

Use the TAB key to move the edit cursor from the "cells:" field to the "alignment:" field. When the cursor moves to a new field, it always highlights the active option. Changing an option in a field is the same as in the main command menu: press the space bar or BACKSPACE key to move forward or backward within the field, or press the first letter of the option that you wish to select. Move the edit cursor over Ctr (for "center"), and press the TAB key. Ctr is now enclosed in parentheses, (Ctr), and the edit cursor has moved to the "format code:" field. For now, you don't need to change any format codes or the number of decimals, so press the TAB key twice to move the edit cursor to the "cells:" field.

The edit cursor now highlights R4C2. Press F9 and the cursor shortens and highlights only the R. Now press the DEL key twice to delete the row reference R4, and only the column reference C2 will be left. If you prefer, you can simply type in **C2**; typing a character automatically erases the default entry. You now have what is required, so press ENTER and notice how the entries in column 2 change. Now do the same for the remaining three columns. Your screen should look like Figure 2-3.

Aligning Decimals

Now align the decimals in the games behind (GB) column. With the command menu on the screen, move the cell pointer to R5C5 and press **Format**. The edit cursor is over the subcommand Cells, which is the one you want to use, so press ENTER. Next reduce the contents of the "cells:" field to C5, either by pressing F9 and then the DEL key twice, or by typing **C5**. Press the TAB key to move to the "alignment:" field and press **Ctr**. Again press the TAB key to move to the "format code:" field and press **Fix**. Fix displays numbers with a fixed number of places after the decimal point. Now press the TAB key to move the edit cursor to the "# of decimals:" field and type **1**. Press ENTER and notice in column 5 that all the numbers are displayed to the tenths place and that all the decimal points are aligned. Your worksheet should look like Figure 2-1 minus the table titles.

Entering Titles

Now all of the data appears as it should, and all that remains to be done is to enter the titles NATIONAL LEAGUE and WEST DIVISION. Each of these titles is longer than the longest entry in column 1, so how will you get them to read in full without making the columns needlessly wide? Multiplan makes it easy to enter titles by allowing you to make rows continuous; they need not be split into columns. That is, the contents of one cell can read across columns to the right, if these columns are blank.

1. Press the HOME key to move the cell pointer to R1C1.
2. Press **Format**, and then, with the edit cursor over the subcommand Cells, press ENTER.
3. Delete C1 from the "cells:" field so all that remains is R1.
4. With the TAB key move the cursor to the "format code:" field and press **Cont** (for "continuous"). Press ENTER.

Row 1 is now set up as a continuous cell, and text of any length up to 150

```
               1            2      3      4       5
 1
 2
 3
 4                          W      L      Pct.    GB
 5 Los Angeles             81     59     0.579    0
 6 Atlanta                 79     61     0.564    2
 7 Houston                 73     66     0.525    7.5
 8 San Diego               70     72     0.493    12
 9 San Francisco           67     74     0.475    14.5
10 Cincinnati              64     78     0.451    18
```

Figure 2-3. *Table with data centered*

characters may be entered and it will all be displayed.

5. Move the cell pointer to R1C2 and press ENTER to select the Alpha command.

6. Type **NATIONAL LEAGUE** and press ENTER.

Even though the cell width for column 2 is only six characters, you have made row 1 continuous so the whole entry, NATIONAL LEAGUE, is displayed on the screen.

7. Move the cell pointer to row 2 and use the same procedure to make row 2 continuous.

8. Move the cell pointer to R2C2 and press ENTER.

9. Type **WEST DIVISION** and again press ENTER.

(You can in fact make a row continuous without moving the cell pointer to that row. Simply type in the desired row in the "cells:" field and follow the previous directions from there.)

The titles are now entered, but their alignment is not correct. To center the titles, move the cell pointer to R1C2 and press ENTER to display ALPHA: NATIONAL LEAGUE on the command line. Now press the F9 key so that the edit cursor highlights only the N of NATIONAL, press the space bar to insert four or five spaces before the text, and press ENTER. Use the same procedure in row 2 to align WEST DIVISION. You can add or delete spaces to center the titles over the table columns. When deleting spaces, be careful that you press F9 to move the edit cursor to the far left of the cell entry before you press the DEL key. If the edit cursor covers NATIONAL LEAGUE when you press DEL, the entire entry will be deleted. Practice deleting and inserting spaces before the titles to get used to this operation. Of course, you need not add these spaces as a separate step. You can add them before you type the entry; once in ALPHA, press the space bar the desired number of times before typing your text.

Saving a Worksheet

The baseball standings table is complete for now, but you should save the worksheet on disk so you can return to it later.

Transfer/Save

To save a worksheet, return to the command menu and press **Transfer**. You are presented with the new command menu:

TRANSFER: <u>Load</u> Save Clear Delete Options Rename

You need the Save command, so press **S**ave or press the space bar and then ENTER. The command line now displays the current filename:

TRANSFER SAVE filename: TEMP

At this time you can change the filename to whatever you choose. Use the name BB.MP — BB for "baseball" and MP to identify it as a Multiplan file. When you type the first character, the filename TEMP will automatically disappear. After typing **BB.MP**, press ENTER.

More information on the Transfer subcommands is given in Chapter 4.

Returning to PC DOS

After you save your worksheet, Multiplan returns you to the screen with the full command menu displayed.

Quit

To quit Multiplan and return to PC DOS, select Quit from the command menu by pressing **Q**. The message line displays

Enter Y to confirm

You must now press **Y** (Yes) to confirm that you really want to quit the Multiplan program. This precaution is built-in because once you quit Multiplan, your worksheet is lost unless you have previously saved it on disk. Pressing any key except **Y** returns you to the command menu and leaves your worksheet intact.

Exercises

1. Review the ways of selecting commands from the command line and practice them. Notice the message that appears on the message line for the command selected. Remember, you can always press the ESC key to return to the command line if you do not wish to complete a command.

2. Enter the data from the following table into a new worksheet. Leave all of Multiplan's options as default values. Use the Alpha command to enter the heights, and do not use the " key; instead press ' twice.

Alhambra Basketball Team

Name	Age	Height	Position	Grade	Avg/Game
ADAMS, T	17	5'11"	F	11	13.4
CAMPBELL, J	16	5'10"	G	12	8.4
LITTLE, M	17	5'9"	G	11	9.5
RUTZ, W	16	6'1"	F	12	16.7
WILSON, A	17	6'4"	C	12	12.6

3. Use the FORMAT WIDTH command to change the column widths in the table so the result closely resembles the example above.

4. Reenter the values in the age column by using the Alpha command (or Value if you used Alpha the first time), and note how the line justification changes.

5. Use the FORMAT cells command to align the decimals in the Avg/Game column. Print one place after the decimal.

Referencing Rows, Columns, and Cells

- Absolute Reference of Cells
- Editing Cell References in the Command Line
- Entering a Pattern
- Erasing Data
- Absolute Reference of Multiple Groups of Cells
- Relative Reference of Cells
- Deleting Rows and Columns

Commands

- COPY FROM
- COPY RIGHT
- COPY DOWN
- Blank
- DELETE COLUMN
- DELETE ROW

In all the worksheets you create, you will be referring to cells — either individually or in groups. For example, you may want to add a column of numbers in your worksheet or to multiply the contents of one cell by the contents of a second cell. To perform these operations, and others like them, you need to have the tools to identify, or *reference,* those cells. There are three ways to do this in Multiplan: (1) absolute reference, (2) relative reference, and (3) name reference. You'll read about absolute reference and relative reference in this chapter and name reference in Chapter 4.

Absolute Reference of Cells

Absolute reference identifies a cell by row and column number. You use absolute reference in its simplest form when you refer to a single cell with the notation $RxCy$, where x and y stand for numbers. You can also use absolute reference to identify a group of cells. Refer to Figure 3-1 during the following discussion.

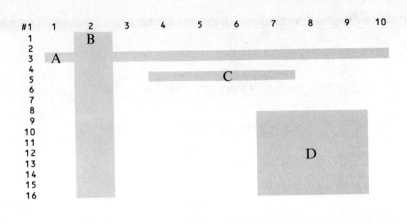

Figure 3-1.   *Absolute reference of cells*

Four areas, or groups of cells, are indicated by shading in the figure. Area A indicates all of row 3, or R3. Though only ten columns are shown in the figure, referencing a row includes the entire row—all 63 columns. Area B represents column 2, or C2—all 255 rows of it. Area C represents a portion of row 5 starting at column 4 and ending at column 7. There are two ways to designate this area: R5C4:R5C7 and R5C4:7. The colon used in these references is called the *range operator*. The range operator separates the two cell locations that identify the boundaries of the references. R5C4:R5C7 refers to all cells in the range from R5C4 through R5C7. R5C4:7 refers to the same cells in row 5 starting at C4 and extending through C7. As you develop worksheets you will see that one method of referring to a range of cells may be preferred over the other in different situations. Both methods will be used in this book.

The fourth area, area D, is a *block* of cells, a group of cells in the shape of a square or rectangle. Like area C, area D can be designated in either of two ways. Just as a portion of a row is identifed by the numbers of its first and last cells (again, R5C4:7, for example), a block of cells is identified by the cells at the opposite ends of either diagonal. Standard practice is to use the diagonal from the upper-left to the lower-right corner—R9C7:R16C9. The second way is to designate area D by identifying the positions of the row and the column that make up that block. That is, area D extends from row 9 through row 16 and from column 7 through column 9, and so is referenced as R9:16C7:9. The row and column ranges are identified by range operators (hence there are two range operators), and the two ranges are written together with no spaces or other punctuation separating them.

Editing Cell References in the Command Line

As you have seen in the previous chapter, many of Multiplan's commands require that you type in or modify references to cells. You do so by using the DELETE key and the function keys F7, F8, F9, and F10.

Copy/From

Let's use the Copy command to practice editing cell references. With the command menu displayed and the cell pointer in the home position, press Copy to get the subcommand line

COPY <u>Right</u> Down From

Press **F** to select the From subcommand. You are presented with the following command line:

COPY FROM cells: <u>R1C1</u>   to cells:R1C1

The edit cursor is over R1C1 in the first "cells:" field. Both fields display the current active cell reference. Press F8 and note that the edit cursor is now after the C1 of the first cell reference. Press F7 and it returns to its original position, over R1C1. The function keys F7 and F8 move the edit cursor "word" left and "word" right, or to cell, row, or column reference. Press F7 and F8 alternately to see how the edit cursor changes.

The function keys F9 and F10 move the edit cursor one character left or right. With the cursor after C1 in the cell reference, press F9 and note that the cursor is just over the 1. Alternately press these keys and note how the cursor moves. With these function keys you can change just those parts of a cell reference that need changing.

Pressing the DEL key deletes whatever is under the edit cursor. Place the cursor over the C of R1C1 and press the DEL key; the C is gone, leaving R11. Press the F7 key so the edit cursor covers R11, and press the DEL key; all that remains is the edit cursor itself.

Reinstate R1C1 by pressing the HOME key. With the edit cursor over R1C1, press the DEL key, and the entire cell reference is deleted. Press the HOME key again.

Pressing one of the four arrow keys to move the cell pointer will change the cell number in the command line as the active cell changes. Press the right arrow key and R1C2 appears as the cell reference; press the HOME key and R1C1 is displayed. Move the cell pointer around the screen and note how the active cell reference changes on the command line.

Entering a Pattern

You can use the Copy command to enter a pattern into a block occupying the first ten rows and columns of the worksheet. On your screen the pattern will look like that in Figure 3-2.

To see the whole pattern on the screen, you need to have ten columns visible, which means you first have to change the column width as you did in Chapter 2. You'll narrow the first ten columns to the minimum width, three characters. To do this, exit the Copy command by pressing ESC and then select the FORMAT WIDTH command. Using the TAB key to move the edit cursor from field to field, enter field values as shown in the next line.

FORMAT WIDTH in char or d(efault):3   column: 1   through: 10

Press ENTER.

The asterisk that makes up this pattern should be treated like text. The command cursor is on Alpha, so press ENTER. Now type an asterisk and press ENTER.

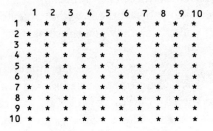

Figure 3-2.   *The pattern to be entered*

Copy/Right

From the command line choose **C**opy and you are presented with the COPY subcommand menu:

COPY: <u>Right</u> Down From

You have three options: COPY RIGHT allows you to copy data from one cell into cells to the right of it in the same row; COPY DOWN allows you to copy data from a cell to cells below it in the same column; and COPY FROM allows you to copy data from a cell or a block of cells to any cell or block of cells in the worksheet. You're going to work with each of these subcommands.

First copy the asterisk to the right. The edit cursor is over the appropriate command, Right, so press ENTER. The command line now reads

COPY RIGHT number of cells: __   starting at: R1C1

Type **9** in the "number of cells:" field. The "starting at:" field contains the current active cell location. Since the asterisk to be copied is located there, this field reference is correct. Press ENTER. The asterisk is copied in the nine columns beyond the starting location, and so the screen displays asterisks in columns 1 through 10 of row 1.

Copy/Down

The next step is to copy the asterisk *down* nine rows. Press **C**opy, and with the subcommand menu displayed, press **D**own. The COPY DOWN command line contains the correct responses from your previous entry:

COPY DOWN number of cells: 9   starting at:R1C1

Press ENTER. Your screen now has asterisks in column 1 from row 1 through row 10 as shown in Figure 3-3.

Copy/From

Now complete the pattern to make a 10 × 10 rectangle of asterisks on the screen. This time you'll copy to the entire block, R2:10C2:10.

1. Again press **C**opy, and from the subcommand menu press **F**rom.

The "FROM cells:" field shows R1C1, which is fine since it contains the asterisk you want to copy.

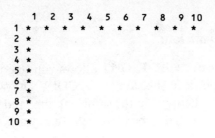

Figure 3-3. *Copy right and Copy down*

   2. Press the TAB key to move to the "to cells:" field.

You can enter the range in one of two ways: either type it in (**R2:10C2:10**) or do the following:

   3. With the command cursor in the "to cells:" field, move the cell pointer to R2C2 and type a colon.

The "to cells:" field displays R2C2:__.

   4. Press the END key to move the cell pointer to R10C10.

The command line now reads

   COPY FROM cells: R1C1   to cells: R2C2:R10C10

The COPY FROM command you have just entered tells Multiplan to copy whatever data is in cell R1C1 into the rectangular block of cells R2 through R10 and C2 through C10.

   5. Press ENTER. Note that the rectangle fills with asterisks. The pattern is now complete.

A couple of additional points: first, the "FROM cells:" field could have referred to any cell that contained an asterisk; second, the reference in the "to cells:" field, R1C1, did not have to be changed to R2C2. Copying asterisks over existing asterisks would not have changed the final result.

Erasing Data

Now let's eliminate a block of asterisks from the center of the 10×10 pattern. You do this with the Blank command.

Blank

Move the cell pointer to R3C3. Press **B**lank and the command line reads

BLANK cells: <u>R3C3</u>

The edit cursor is over the single cell reference R3C3, but you need to enter a *range*. To do this, simply type in :, the range operator, and the edit cursor automatically moves to the right of the cell reference. The command line will look like this:

BLANK cells: R3C3: __

You can type in the range, or if you are working with a relatively small section of the worksheet, you can use another method: move the cell pointer to R8C8. Notice that as you move the pointer, the command line always shows its position following the colon. Your command line reads as follows:

BLANK cells: R3C3:R8C8

Now press ENTER and the cells in the indicated block are blanked. The screen should look like Figure 3-4.

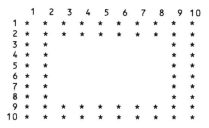

Figure 3-4. *Screen after use of Blank*

Let's fill in the screen again with the 10 × 10 array of asterisks.

1. Move the cell pointer to R2C2 (it can be over any asterisk).
2. Select the COPY FROM command (press Copy, then From).
3. Use the TAB key to move to the "to cells:" field.
4. Move the cell pointer to R3C3, type a colon, and move the cell pointer to R8C8.

The command line displays the following:

COPY FROM cells: R2C2   to cells: R3C3:R8C8

Press ENTER and the block pattern is again complete.

Now clear the worksheet, again using the Blank command.

1. Place the cell pointer in the home position and press Blank.
2. Type a colon and then press the END key to move the cell pointer to the outermost cell that's been used on the worksheet (in this case, R10C10).
3. Press ENTER and the entire worksheet should be blanked.

Absolute Reference of Multiple Groups of Cells

Multiplan has a *union operator,* the comma, that allows you to reference individual cells that are not connected or two or more blocks of cells in one operation. Figure 3-5 shows three groups of cells. The area A range is R3C2:R10C3, the area B range is R5C1:R7C6, and the area C range is R9C7:R10C9. Although blocks A and B intersect, having cells in common, they can be dealt with as separate groups. Using the comma to separate areas enables you to reference all three areas in one command, like this:

R3C2:R10C3,R5C1:R7C6,R9C7:R10C9

To practice this method of referencing cells, let's enter asterisks in a pattern created by the three blocks shown in Figure 3-5. Move the cell pointer to R3C2 and enter an asterisk. Press Copy and From. Move the edit cursor to the "to cells:" field and enter the absolute references to the three areas, separating each area reference with a comma. The completed command line should look like this:

COPY FROM cells: R3C2   to cells: R3C2:R10C3,R5C1:R7C6,R9C7:R10C9

Press ENTER, and your screen will look like the example shown in Figure 3-6.

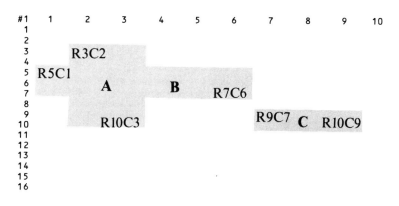

Figure 3-5.   *Multiple groups of cells to be linked by the union operator*

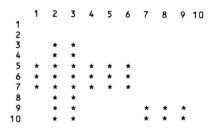

Figure 3-6.   *Result of the union operator*

Notice that the screen display is not affected by the cell references that overlap. Also, the number of cell references that you may enter is limited only by the length of the command line.

Relative Reference of Cells

Relative referencing is one of Multiplan's most useful, powerful, and challenging concepts. It allows you to refer to cells, called *target* cells, by their position in relation to a given cell, called the *source* cell. Given one source cell, let's use relative referencing to refer to other cells and groups of cells. Refer to Figure 3-7 during the following discussion.

The source cell is R5C5. There are three targets; T1 and T2 are cells and T3 is a block of cells. T1, the first target cell, is R3C3 (as identified by absolute reference). You can see on the worksheet that R3C3 is two rows above and two columns to the left of the source cell. Using relative referencing you indicate the target cell relative to the source cell as R[−2]C[−2].

In relative referencing, the row and column positions relative to the source cell are given in brackets. A row *above* the source has a smaller number and thus a negative reference, such as R[−2]; a column to the *left* also has a smaller number and a negative reference, such as C[−2]. Rows and columns below or to the right of the source cell have larger numbers and thus have positive references, such as R[+2] and C[+2]. A relative reference on the same row or column as the source cell needs no brackets at all; for example, a target cell on the same row as the source cell and two columns to the right of it would be RC[+2], and a target cell in the same column as the source cell and two rows below it would be R[+2]C.

The second target in Figure 3-7, T2, is at R2C6. It is three rows above and one

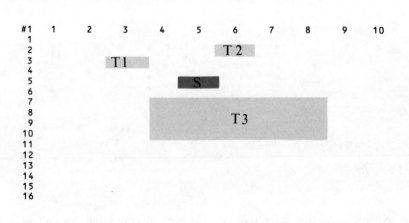

Figure 3-7. *Relative reference of cells. A source, R5C5, and three targets, T1, T2, and T3*

column to the right of the source cell, so it is referenced as R[−3]C[+1].

A convenient way to experiment with this relationship between absolute and relative reference is to use the Value command. Blank your worksheet and place the cell pointer in R1C1. Enter the Value command. Now, with the arrow keys, move the cell pointer about the screen and notice two things: the command line displays the position of the cell pointer relative to R1C1, and the status line displays the absolute position of the cell pointer. (What will the command line display if you move the cell pointer back to R1C1?)

Like absolute references, relative references make use of the range operator to identify a block of cells. Looking at Figure 3-7, you can see that in relation to the source cell, the upper-left corner of the target block, T3, is two rows down and one column to the left, and the lower-right corner is five rows down and three columns to the right—that is, the target block T3 can be referenced as R[+2]C[−1]:R[+5]C[+3].

Let's copy asterisks into each of the target areas indicated in Figure 3-7.

1. Blank your worksheet and move the cell pointer to R5C5, the source cell.
2. Enter an asterisk.
3. Select the COPY FROM command.
4. Move the edit cursor to the "to cells:" field.
5. Type in the location of T1 using relative reference notation.

The command line looks like this:

COPY FROM cells: R5C5   to cells: R[−2]C[−2]

6. Press ENTER and the asterisk is copied to the target cell R3C3.

Follow the same procedure to copy the contents of the source cell into target cell T2. To copy the asterisk into target area T3, enter the target cells as shown above. The command line should look like this:

COPY FROM cells: R5C5   to cells:R[+2]C[−1]:R[+5]C[+3]

Press ENTER and your screen looks like the example shown in Figure 3-8.

A note of caution: Be careful not to mix relative reference with absolute reference when referring to a *single cell*. For example, typing in the following reference will give you an "error in formula" message in the message line, and the edit cursor will move to the reference that caused the error.

R10C[−2] ← Wrong
R10C3 or R[+5]C[−2] ← Right

You *can* combine relative and absolute references when you refer to *different* cells. For example, you can copy R5C5 to R[+2]C[+3]:R5C3.

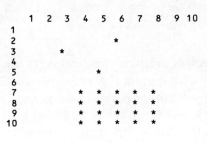

Figure 3-8.   *Screen after use of relative cell references*

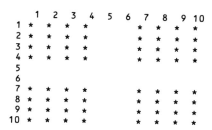

Figure 3-9.   *Screen after using Blank*

Deleting Rows and Columns

Now blank your screen and again enter the 10 × 10 array of asterisks in R1C1:R10C10. Before you use the Delete command, blank rows 5 and 6 and columns 5 and 6 to make the pattern shown in Figure 3-9. To blank the columns, you enter this command line:

   BLANK cells: C5:6

To blank the rows, you enter

   BLANK cells: R5:6

Delete

   Now let's use the Delete command.

   1. Press **D**elete and the command line displays

DELETE: <u>Row</u> Column

   2. Since the edit cursor is on the proper command, Row, press ENTER.

If the cell pointer was in the home position, you now have the following command lines:

DELETE ROW # of rows: <u>1</u>   starting at: 1
        between columns: 1   and: 63

   3. In the "# of rows:" field type **2**.

4. With the TAB key move to the "starting at:" field, type 5, and press ENTER.

Watch the screen as you press ENTER and notice how the pattern closes up because rows have been deleted.

Next, use the DELETE COLUMN command to delete columns 5 and 6.

5. Press **D**elete and **C**olumn. Fill in the fields as follows:

DELETE COLUMN # of columns: 2   starting at: 5
                between rows: 1   and: 255

6. Press ENTER and notice that two columns of asterisks are deleted.

Your worksheet should now display the solid 8×8 pattern of asterisks shown in Figure 3-10.

Now try a more defined example of the Delete command, in which you specify cells within a range of rows *and* columns to be deleted.

Select the DELETE ROW command and fill in the fields so your command line looks like this:

DELETE ROW # of rows: 2   starting at: 5
              between columns: 3   and: 6

Be sure to fill in the two fields on the second line. Before pressing ENTER, look at the command line and consider what will happen to your screen display when you execute this command. Press ENTER. Were you correct? A block of cells should have been deleted in the center of the worksheet, and those asterisks below the block moved up to close up the space. Your display looks like Figure 3-11.

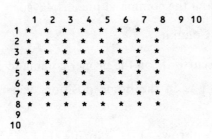

Figure 3-10.   *Screen after using Delete on rows and columns*

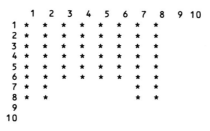

Figure 3-11.   *Deleting partial rows*

Many Multiplan tools were introduced in this chapter, and you will use them throughout your work with the program. In the next chapter you'll use these tools in more practical applications.

Exercises

1. Enter a 10 × 10 block of asterisks like the one you worked with in this chapter.

2. Produce the following pattern. Use the Blank command in conjunction with the union operator (comma) to remove the four corners of the block with one command.

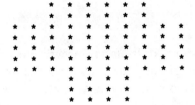

3. Use the Delete command to reduce the pattern as follows:

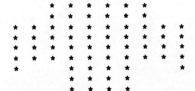

4. Finallly, use the Delete command to obtain this pattern:

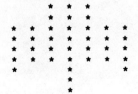

Using Formulas

- Loading Files
- Planning Calculations
- Building a Formula
- Naming Cells
- Using Names in Formulas
- Clearing the Worksheet
- Building Formulas — A Review

Commands

- TRANSFER LOAD
- Name
- TRANSFER CLEAR

Now that you've had some practice with Multiplan's commands and with referencing cells, let's return to the baseball worksheet that you entered in Chapter 2. You'll use this background to build the formulas necessary for Multiplan to calculate the results of the Pct. (percentage) and GB (games behind) columns.

Loading Files

In order to work with the baseball worksheet, you have to load Multiplan and transfer the program from the disk to the computer's memory. For this you load Multiplan and then, when the worksheet is displayed, you use the Transfer command. (Transfer is the same command you use to save the worksheet on disk.)

43

Transfer/Load

Press **T**ransfer to get the TRANSFER menu:

TRANSFER: <u>Load</u> Save Clear Delete Options Rename

The edit cursor is over the Load command, which is what you want, so press ENTER. The following command line is displayed:

TRANSFER LOAD filename: —

To name the file you want transferred from the disk to the computer and displayed on the screen, you can do one of two things. You can type in the name, such as BB.MP, or you can press the right arrow key, causing the directory of your logged disk to be displayed.

Let's try the second method: press the right arrow key and the directory of your disk should be displayed across the top few rows of the screen. Your directory will be different, but the layout will be like this:

```
COMMAND  COM  MP      SYS  LESSON1  WE  LESSON2 WE
BB            MP  STOCK  MP  BBNAME   MP
```

The directory cursor is over the file in the home position. Move the cursor with the arrow keys, just as you move the cell pointer, to highlight the name of the file you wish to load. The END key moves the cursor to the last filename, and the HOME key returns it to the home position from any position in the directory. Practice moving the directory cursor over the various filenames, and notice as you do that the filename in the command line changes to match the filename highlighted by the directory cursor.

(When your disk directory becomes large, it can become time-consuming to spot the file you wish to load. Multiplan offers a way to limit the number of filenames that are displayed by the method just described: you use the asterisk as a "wildcard" to represent any letter or group of letters. For example, if you press **Transfer** and **Load**, and in the "filename:" field you type **∗.MP** and press the right arrow key, your screen will display only those files that have the extension MP. If you type **PH∗.∗** in the "filename:" field and press the right arrow key, only those files starting with the letters PH will be displayed. You then select the file you want as outlined in the previous paragraph.)

To load the baseball program, move the directory cursor over BB.MP and press ENTER.

Planning Calculations

All the data in this worksheet was entered in Chapter 2 on the keyboard. Now you'll take advantage of Multiplan's calculation abilities to determine the results for the last two columns. (You could, of course, just enter the appropriate numbers and calculate the percentage for each team; but the real power of Multiplan comes from using its referencing capabilities to build formulas that can be copied into all the required cells.)

First, blank the data from the last two columns of the worksheet. To do this, move the cell pointer to R5C4 and press **B**lank. Type in **:**, the range operator, and press the END key to move the *cell pointer* to the last active cell on your worksheet. Your command line looks like this:

BLANK cells: R5C4:R10C5

Press ENTER to blank the cells indicated. Your screen should look like Figure 4-1.

Before Multiplan determines percentage and games behind, you need to consider the formulas involved. First you will do the Pct. column. The percent of games won is determined by the following formula:

$$\frac{\text{Games won}}{\text{Total games played}}$$

In this formula Total games played = Games won + Games lost. The formula may then be written as

$$\frac{\text{Games won}}{\text{Games won} + \text{Games lost}}$$

	1	2	3	4	5
1			NATIONAL LEAGUE		
2			WEST DIVISION		
3					
4		W	L	Pct.	GB
5	Los Angeles	81	59		
6	Atlanta	79	61		
7	Houston	73	66		
8	San Diego	70	72		
9	San Francisco	67	74		
10	Cincinnati	64	78		

Figure 4-1. *Table ready to receive formulas*

Now substitute into this formula the information particular to the Los Angeles team.

$$\frac{81}{81 + 59}$$

This formula can be written as $81/(81+59)$. It can also be written in Multiplan's relative reference notation as

$$RC[-2]/(RC[-2]+RC[+1])$$

Thus, the relationship between the relative reference of Multiplan's notation and the particular data for the Los Angeles team can be expressed as

$$\underbrace{RC[-2]}_{81} / \underbrace{(RC[-2]+RC[-1])}_{(81 + 59)}$$

Building a Formula

Now enter the Multiplan formula, $RC[-2]/(RC[-2]+RC[-1])$, into the worksheet. When building a formula, you start with the cell pointer in the cell where you want the results to appear.

Move the cell pointer to R5C4, the first cell in which the formula will be used. Formulas are treated as numeric data, so press **Value**. Use the left arrow key to move the cell pointer two columns to the left, to the W (games won) column. The command line should show this relative reference:

VALUE: $RC[-2]$—

This is the correct cell reference, so proceed to enter the formula. Type in the division symbol, /, and the left parenthesis, (. As soon as you type /, the cell pointer moves back to R5C4. It will do so each time you enter a mathematical operator. Again move the cell pointer two columns to the left, to the W column, and enter a plus sign, +. Again the cell pointer returns to R5C4. Now move the cell pointer one column to the left to the L (games lost) column, and enter the right parenthesis,).

The formula is now complete and the command line displays

VALUE: $RC[-2]/(RC[-2]+RC[-1])$

This matches the previous formula. Press ENTER and the result of the calculation is displayed in cell R5C4 as shown in Figure 4-2.

In Figure 2-1 of Chapter 2 the results in the Pct. column are shown to three places after the decimal. To set the decimals in column 4 of the new table to three places, use the FORMAT cells command. In the "cells:" field enter **C4**; with the TAB key move the command cursor to the "Format code:" field and select **F**ix. Finally, move the command cursor to the "# of decimals:" field and type **3**. Your command line displays the following:

FORMAT cells: C4   alignment:(Def)Ctr Gen Left Right —
format code: Def Cont Exp(Fix)Gen Int $ * % —   # of decimals: 3

Press ENTER and 0.579 appears in R5C4.

Copying Formulas Using Relative Referencing

The same formula determines the percentage for each of the other teams. Because you used relative referencing, however, you do not have to enter the formula again. You merely copy it in the Pct. column for the remaining teams.

With the cell pointer still in R5C4, press **C**opy. You want to copy down, so press **D**. There are five additional teams, so enter **5** in the "number of cells:" field. This command line appears:

COPY DOWN number of cells: 5   starting at: R5C4

The cell reference in the "starting at:" field is correct, so press ENTER. The correct results are now complete in column 4, just as they were when you typed them in on the keyboard in Chapter 2.

Now you can turn to the GB (games behind) column and determine those values. To do this, you need a formula that tells the number of games by which

	1	2	3	4	5
1			NATIONAL LEAGUE		
2			WEST DIVISION		
3					
4		W	L	Pct.	GB
5	Los Angeles	81	59	0.5785714	
6	Atlanta	79	61		
7	Houston	73	66		
8	San Diego	70	72		
9	San Francisco	67	74		
10	Cincinnati	64	78		

Figure 4-2. *Formula calculated to the default number of decimal places*

each team is behind the leading team. You construct the formula by adding the difference between the two teams in games won and the difference between them in games lost and dividing by two; that is:

Games Behind = (Leader's Games Won − Games WON + Games LOST − Leader's Games Lost) / 2

As a specific example, insert the data for the Atlanta team. Adding the data to the formula for the leading team (Los Angeles) and Atlanta yields the following:

$$\frac{(81-79) + (61-59)}{2} \quad \text{or} \quad ((81-79) + (61-59))/2$$

Multiplan can now subtract the games won by Atlanta from the games won by Los Angeles, and it can subtract the games lost by Los Angeles from the games lost by Atlanta. To build a formula that does this for more than one pair of teams, you must combine relative and absolute cell references. The performance figures for each team being compared to the leading team are on a different row — for example, Atlanta's are on row 6, San Francisco's on row 9 — so relative cell references are used in the formula to enable the formula to be copied for each team. However, the leading team's values for games won and games lost are in two unchanging cells, R5C2 and R5C3. These must be absolute cell references in the formula. Thus, the formula for games behind is constructed of the following notation:

((R5C2− RC[−3])+(RC[−2]− R5C3))/2

The second, outside set of parentheses in this formula is used just to group the numbers, but is not needed for obtaining correct results. Without the extra parentheses, the formula is written as

(R5C2− RC[−3]+ RC[−2]− R5C3)/2

Enter this simpler version into the worksheet.

1. Move the cell pointer to R5C5 and press Value.
2. Type the first character of the formula, (.

You could now type in the absolute reference to cell R5C2, but follow steps 3 and 4 instead.

3. Use the left arrow key to move the cell pointer three columns to the left, over the 81 in the W (games won) column.

Notice that your command line reads (RC[−3].

4. Press the F3 key.

Notice that the cell reference changes immediately from relative reference to the absolute reference R5C2, which is the first value in the formula. Your command line now displays the following:

VALUE: (R5C2_

5. Type −.

6. Move the cursor three columns to the left, to the W column, and type +.

7. Move the cell pointer two columns to the left, to the L column, and type the last −.

8. Move the cursor two columns to the left and press F3 to change the cell number to absolute reference, R5C3.

9. Type (, /, and **2**.

Your command line now displays the following:

VALUE: (R5C2− RC[−3]+ RC[−2]− R5C3)/2

This is the formula you want, so

10. Press ENTER.

Cell R5C5 shows 0.0, which is correct for the leading team.

This formula can be copied down five rows to calculate the number of games the other teams are behind. Press **C**opy and **D**own. The command line shows the correct reference in the "number of cells:" field and the "starting at:" field, so press ENTER and the GB column will be complete as shown in Figure 4-3.

The advantage of having formulas in the percentage and games behind columns is that when you update a team's games won and games lost standings,

	1	2	3	4	5
1			NATIONAL LEAGUE		
2			WEST DIVISION		
3					
4		W	L	Pct.	GB
5 Los Angeles		81	59	0.579	0.0
6 Atlanta		79	61	0.564	2.0
7 Houston		73	66	0.525	7.5
8 San Diego		70	72	0.493	12.0
9 San Francisco		67	74	0.475	14.5
10 Cincinnati		64	78	0.451	18.0

Figure 4-3. *Table with formulas entered and copies, and with decimal places set*

the PCT. and GB statistics will be recalculated automatically. As an example, change the number of games won by San Francisco to 70 (move the pointer to R9C2, type **70**, and press ENTER). Note how the games won, percentage, and games behind values change for the San Francisco team. (At this stage you would have to rearrange the teams manually if new entries in the won and lost columns were to change the division standings. As you learn more about Multiplan, you will acquire additional tools to help you perform any such rearrangements.)

Before you move on to learn another way of entering formulas, save this example. Press Transfer and Save. You now have the option of changing the name of the worksheet. This worksheet was previously saved as BB.MP, which is what the command line displays. But let's change the name to BBC4.MP to indicate that the worksheet was done in Chapter 4 and is different in construction from the one in Chapter 2.

To change the filename you can either type in the new one from scratch or insert the characters **C4** into the current filename. To do the latter, press F9 once and then F10 twice so your command line and edit cursor display as follows:

TRANSFER SAVE filename: BB.MP

Now type **C4** and it will be inserted before the period. Your command line displays

TRANSFER SAVE filename: BBC4.MP

Press ENTER to save the file under this filename. Note that the original baseball worksheet from Chapter 2 is still on your disk under its original name BB.MP.

Naming Cells

So far you have used absolute and relative referencing to build formulas. Multiplan offers another method of referring to cells: by name. Let's try this now with the baseball worksheet.

Name

In preparation, blank the percentage and games behind columns.

1. Move the cell pointer to the heading of the games won column — over the W in R4C2.
2. Press **Name.** You are presented with the following command line:

NAME: define name: W   to refer to: R4C2

In the "define name:" field, Multiplan suggests by default that you use the name of whatever text is in the active cell. Normally this is the best procedure, but here a more descriptive name, such as WON, is appropriate.

3. Type **WON** in this field.
4. Either type in **R4:10C2** from scratch or press F9; then press F10 twice and type **:10**.

Your command line now displays

NAME: define name: WON   to refer to: R4:10C2

5. Press ENTER.

There is no visible change in the worksheet, but Multiplan will remember the name WON and the cells it refers to.

6. Now move the active cell pointer over the L in the games lost column.
7. Press **Name.**
8. Type the name **LOST** for the values in this column.

Note that the "to refer to:" field now contains the correct reference, R4:10C3. This is because Multiplan retains the same value used in the last entry, adjusted for the change in column number.

9. Press ENTER.

Using Names in Formulas

Names can be useful in formulas. Let's see how the WON and LOST names are used in the percentage and games behind formulas of the baseball table. To enter a name in a formula you use the F3 key (the same key that is used to change relative references to absolute references).

Begin with the percentage column. Remember, the formula can be stated as

$$\text{Percentage} = \frac{\text{Games WON}}{\text{Games WON} + \text{Games LOST}}$$

or

$$\text{Percentage} = \text{Games WON} / (\text{Games WON} + \text{Games LOST})$$

1. Move the cell pointer to the first data cell of the percentage column, R5C4.
2. Press Value.
3. Press the F3 key and then the right arrow key.

Pressing these two keys causes cell names to be displayed on the command line; they do not cause the cell pointer to move.

The first name you used was WON, so it is now displayed in the command line. You change the name displayed by pressing either the left or right arrow key to step forward or backward through the entire worksheet names list. (Note that only one name in the list is shown at a time.) In this instance there are only two names.

4. Press the right and left arrow keys to see how the name changes.

At times you may have a long list of names assigned to data or text in your worksheet. You can use the HOME key to go to the beginning of the list and the END key to go to its end, and then use the right and left arrow keys to move forward or backward within the list.

You want to enter WON in the percentage formula. To do this,

5. Display WON on the command line.
6. Type /.
7. Type (.
8. Press F3 and the right arrow to display the cell names again.

9. Display WON on the command line.
10. Type **+**.

Now you need to enter the last cell name in the formula.

11. Press F3 and then press the right arrow key twice to display the cell name LOST.
12. Conclude the formula by typing **)**.

Your command line now looks like this:

VALUE: WON/(WON+LOST)

13. Press ENTER.

The calculations of the first team's percentage of wins are displayed on the worksheet. Now, just as you did in the previous example, use the Copy command to copy the formula for the five remaining teams.

When you finish, use this same method to enter the formula for determining games behind. The formula is

Games Behind = (Leader's Games Won − Games WON
+ Games LOST − Leader's Games Lost) / 2

1. Move the cell pointer to R5C5 and press **Value**.
2. Type **)**.
3. Move the cell pointer over the 81 in the games won column.

Notice that the command line shows the relative reference. An absolute reference is needed in this part of the formula.

4. Press F3 to change the relative reference to an absolute reference.
5. Type **−**.

You can now use the Name reference.

6. Press F3 and the right arrow key to display the name WON.
7. Type **+**.
8. Again press F3 and then the right arrow key twice to display the name LOST.
9. Type **−**.
10. Move the cell pointer to the games lost column over the 59.
11. Press F3 to convert the relative reference to an absolute reference.
12. Type **)**, **/**, and **2**.

Your command line now reads

Value: (R5C2 − WON + LOST − R5C3)/2

13. Press ENTER.

The result is displayed in R5C5.

Again copy the formula in column 5 to the remaining teams. Then, so you may have an example of formulas built with name references, save this worksheet under the filename BBC4NAME.MP. The worksheet has been saved on disk and remains on screen, but its name has been changed.

Clearing a Worksheet

Your work with the baseball worksheet for this chapter is done. But instead of blanking the screen, you can use the TRANSFER CLEAR command to prepare for a new worksheet.

Transfer/Clear

The Clear command enables you to clear a worksheet from the computer's memory without quitting Multiplan. When you save a worksheet and want to load or begin another, you can use the TRANSFER CLEAR command to clear the current worksheet from memory. Press **T**ransfer and **C**lear. The following message line appears below the TRANSFER CLEAR command:

Enter Y to confirm —

You must type **Y** in order to execute the command. Pressing any other key will return you to your (unchanged) worksheet.

Besides clearing the screen, the TRANSFER CLEAR command sets the column widths back to the default value of 10, sets the alignment and format fields to default, and resets the worksheet name to TEMP. (However, it does not change the options set with the TRANSFER OPTIONS mode or the PRINT OPTIONS settings; nor does it change those set with the the Options command. You'll learn about all these later in the book.)

Building Formulas — A Review

The last few pages have covered quite a bit of information, so let's look at a short example to recap the different ways of building formulas. Use TRANSFER CLEAR to clear the worksheet. In R1C1 type in the text **NUMBER1**, and in R1C2 type in the text **NUMBER2**. Moving the cell pointer, enter the value **31** in

R4C1 and **63** in R4C2. Your screen will display what is shown in Figure 4-4.

You're now going to find the sum of these two numbers by using the three methods you just learned.

First find the sum by using absolute reference.

1. Move the cell pointer to R3C3 and press **Value**.
2. Next, move the pointer over the 31 and press the F3 key so your relative reference changes to an absolute reference.
3. Type in a plus sign and move the cell pointer over the 63.
4. Again press F3 and then ENTER.

The sum now appears in R3C3, and the status line displays your formula.

Now you use relative reference to find the sum.

5. Move the cell pointer to R4C3 and press **Value**.
6. To enter the formula by using relative reference, move the cell pointer over the 31 and type **+**.
7. Move the cell pointer over the 63 and press ENTER.

Again the sum is displayed.

The next step is to add these numbers by using name references.

8. Press the HOME key to move the cell pointer over NUMBER1.
9. Press **Name**. Use NUMBER1, the default value, for the name.
10. Press the TAB key to move to the "to refer to:" field.
11. With the down arrow key move the cell pointer over the 31.

The command line reads

NAME: define name: NUMBER1   to refer to: R4C1

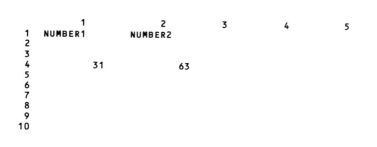

```
                    1              2          3         4          5
      1    NUMBER1         NUMBER2
      2
      3
      4           31              63
      5
      6
      7
      8
      9
     10
```

Figure 4-4. *Table with input ready for calculation*

12. Press ENTER and move the active cell pointer over NUMBER2. Follow the same procedure to make the name NUMBER2 refer to 63.

The command line now reads

NAME: define name: NUMBER2   to refer to: R4C2

13. Press ENTER. Place the cell pointer in R5C3 and press Value.
14. Press F3 and the right arrow key to display the name NUMBER1 on the command line.

VALUE: NUMBER1—

15. Type + and press F3 and the right arrow key twice to display the name NUMBER2 on the command line:

VALUE: NUMBER1+NUMBER2

16. Press ENTER and your screen displays the sum again.

The screen should look like Figure 4-5.

To review the formulas entered into the worksheet, move the cell pointer over each of the sums and the formula will be displayed in the status line.

In each of these formulas you used the same type of reference for both numbers. This is not necessary; you can mix reference types in any one formula as you did in figuring the games behind results for the baseball statistics worksheet. For example, you could place the cell pointer in R6C3 and enter the formula

VALUE:R[−2]C[−2]+ R4C2

Press ENTER and you will again have the sum 94.

	1	2	3	4	5
1	NUMBER1	NUMBER2			
2					
3			94		
4	31	63	94		
5			94		
6					
7					
8					
9					
10					

Figure 4-5. *Table with calculations done by three referencing methods*

A Final Example

To use Multiplan efficiently, you have to master the skills of using relative references and writing formulas. Let's develop one more example before moving on to the next chapter. In preparation, clear the worksheet with the TRANSFER CLEAR command.

Format the worksheet before you enter the data. You're going to enter the 10×10 array shown in Figure 4-6. This array shows a multiplication table for the numbers 1×1 through 10×10.

Row 2 contains the worksheet heading, so it should be continuous. Move the cell pointer to R2C1, and press Format. Since you want the Cells command, press ENTER. Change the reference in the "cells:" field to R2C5:7. With the TAB key, move the edit cursor to the "Format code:" field and press Cont (for "continuous"). Your command line displays the following:

FORMAT cells: R2C5:7   alignment:(Def)Ctr Gen Left Right
      format code: Def <u>Cont</u> Exp Fix Gen Int $ * % — # of decimals:

Press ENTER to execute this command. (Note that you did not format the entire row so it would be continuous, as you did in Chapter 2. The range operator is now available for controlling the section you want formatted. It's a good idea to get in the habit of applying any special formatting only to the required cells. Doing so will help a great deal in maintaining the speed of Multiplan's calculations, especially in large worksheets.)

The column widths should be adjusted to six characters. Press Format and

	1	2	3	4	5	6	7	8	9	10	11
1											
2					TIMES	TABLE					
3											
4	1	2	3	4	5	6	7	8	9	10	
5	2	4	6	8	10	12	14	16	18	20	
6	3	6	9	12	15	18	21	24	27	30	
7	4	8	12	16	20	24	28	32	36	40	
8	5	10	15	20	25	30	35	40	45	50	
9	6	12	18	24	30	36	42	48	54	60	
10	7	14	21	28	35	42	49	56	63	70	
11	8	16	24	32	40	48	56	64	72	80	
12	9	18	27	36	45	54	63	72	81	90	
13	10	20	30	40	50	60	70	80	90	100	

Figure 4-6. *Multiplication table to be built by formula and the Copy command*

Width. Type **6**, move the edit cursor to the "through:" field and type **11**. The command line displays

FORMAT WIDTH in chars or d(efault): 6 column: 1 through: 11

Press ENTER and note how the column widths quickly change.

You can now begin to enter data. To enter the title, move the cell pointer to R2C5; then, to choose the Alpha command, press ENTER. Type the title **TIMES TABLE** and press ENTER.

The numbers 1 through 10 are entered across the top of the table, starting at R4C2. Move the cell pointer to R4C2, type **1**, and press ENTER. You can enter the remaining numbers by using the formula RC[−1]+1. Move the cell pointer to R4C3 and press **Value**. Enter the formula RC[−1]+1. Press ENTER and the number 2 appears in cell R4C3.

Copy this formula in the remaining columns of row 4 (press **Copy** and **Right**). In the "number of cells:" field, type **8**. The "starting at:" field is correct, so press ENTER. The first row of the table is now complete.

Use the same procedure to enter the numbers 1 through 10 in column 2. Move the cell pointer to R5C2 and enter the formula R[−1]C+1. Press ENTER and the number 2 appears in R5C2. Copy the formula down eight rows and your screen display now looks like Figure 4-7.

Now enter the formulas to complete the table. Move the cell pointer to R5C3 and press **Value**. The correct value for this cell is the product of the numbers R4C3 and R5C2. Press the up arrow key, type ∗ (the multiplication symbol), and type **C2**. Your command line reads

VALUE: R[−1]C∗C2

Note that by typing only C2 in this formula, you instruct Multiplan to assume that the value in column 2 is for the row the cell pointer is in — in this case, row 5.

Before you press ENTER, compare this formula with the values it refers to on the screen so you see why it will yield the value 4 in the active cell. Press ENTER.

Now proceed to copy this formula in row 5 to the remaining columns of the table. Move the cell pointer to R6C3 and enter the formula R[−2]C∗C2. Press ENTER. Move to R7C3, enter the formula R[−3]C∗C2, and press ENTER. Each time you move down a row, the number in the brackets changes by 1. When the cell pointer is in R13C3, the formula entered will be R[−9]C∗C2. When you have finished the formulas in column 3, copy them to the remaining eight columns of each row. The table will be complete and should look like the display in Figure 4-6.

With the table now finished, you might try a little experiment. Note that all the references in the table are to the first number you entered, 1, in R4C2. If you

	1	2	3	4	5	6	7	8	9	10	11
1											
2						TIMES	TABLE				
3											
4		1	2	3	4	5	6	7	8	9	10
5		2									
6		3									
7		4									
8		5									
9		6									
10		7									
11		8									
12		9									
13		10									

Figure 4-7. *Partially built table*

change this number, every number in the table will be affected. Try it. Move the cell pointer to R4C2. Press **Value** and type the number **11**. Press ENTER and watch what happens: the entire table changes. You might try this a few more times with other values and note that in the message line, a message tells you how many cells there are to recalculate.

You're through with this worksheet for a while, but you will return to it in a later chapter. To save the worksheet, press **Transfer** and **Save**. Name the program TIMES.C4.

Exercises

1. First, using the TRANSFER LOAD command, load BBNAMEC4.MP into the computer. In R4C6 enter a new heading, TG (for "total games"). Now build a formula with relative references to show the total games played by Los Angeles. Copy the formula into the appropriate cells under TG to produce the correct result for each of the remaining teams.

2. Blank the results you just produced in the TG column. Again build a formula to produce the correct results in the TG column, this time using the Names method.

3. Assign names to the Pct., GB, and TG columns, being sure to refer to the proper column and row so that all teams are included. Use the Name command, the left and right arrow keys, and the HOME and END keys to step through these names.

4. Now save your worksheet under the filename BBMYPROG.MB. Use the appropriate edit keys to change the name with the smallest number of keystrokes.

Printing a Worksheet

- Planning a Worksheet
- Entering a Loan Payment Worksheet
- Using the Print Command
- Printing a File
- Printing Formulas

Commands

- Print/Printer
- PRINT OPTIONS
- PRINT MARGINS

You now have enough working knowledge of the Multiplan program to create useful worksheets. In addition to saving your worksheet onto disk, you will want a *hard copy,* a copy printed on paper.

With the IBM PC you can always print what you see on the screen by pressing the SHIFT and PRTSC keys simultaneously. But normally when you print a worksheet you will want to use Multiplan's Print command, because it allows you to print an entire worksheet or any section of it that you wish. You have several options that enable you to decide exactly what will be printed. These options are introduced later in this chapter, but first let's develop the worksheet you are going to print.

Planning a Worksheet

Suppose you purchase a piece of property on which to build a retirement home. The seller of the property carries the loan. It's up to you to determine the monthly principal, interest, and balance. The financial data that apply to the property are

Purchase date   : March 3, 1983
Purchase price   : $30,000
Down payment   : $5,000
Balance   : $25,000
Interest   : 11%
Monthly payment : $350

The payments are to begin on April 1, 1983, and the balance is to be paid off with a balloon payment at the end of five years.

It's useful to plan a worksheet on paper before entering it into the computer. Figure 5-1 shows an example, the planning information for the RETIREMENT LAND worksheet.

How much planning you do for a worksheet depends largely on how much experience you have with Multiplan. How fast you build your final worksheet depends largely on your planning. You should do as much planning as necessary so you can quickly enter a Multiplan worksheet.

The example in Figure 5-1 is a complete plan. The right column indicates the format for the various sections of the worksheet. The first five rows are formatted to be continuous since they contain most of the titles. Row 6 contains the column headings; the headings in parentheses should be centered, and the underlined headings will be designated by the Name command to be used in the formulas. Since you cannot underline headings in Multiplan, you will enter a row of = marks at row 7 to separate the headings from the data.

The main section of the worksheet is indicated by the rectangle. Since all the data in this section will represent dollars and cents, you will use the Format command Fix 2 to print all the data with two decimal places. The $ shown in cell R4C3 indicates that this cell will be formatted so that the dollar sign and two decimal places print out automatically.

The formulas section of the planning sheet contains all of the formulas that will be used in the final worksheet. Let's consider each of these in turn. Payment is a constant, $350.00, so that is entered down the entire PAYMENT column.

There are three formulas for calculating interest. The first formula describes how the interest is calculated. The second and third are Multiplan formulas. The second, BEGINNING BALANCE*.11/12, is a direct translation of the first formula and will be entered in the top row of the INTEREST column. The third formula, R[−1]C[+2]*.11/12, will be used to calculate interest in the remaining rows.

The formula for calculating principal is followed by the parallel Multiplan formula. Note that the balance calculation also requires two Multiplan formulas, one for the first row and the other for the remaining rows.

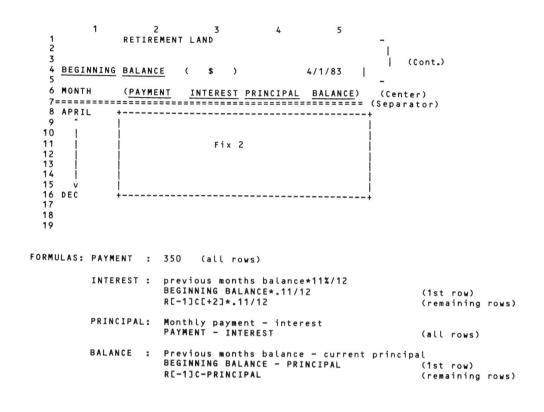

Figure 5-1. *A sample preplanning worksheet*

Entering a Loan Payment Worksheet

Load Multiplan from your disk — do not just use Blank, because if you do, you will carry over any format values from your previous worksheet. If you load from DOS, your command lines will match those shown in the book as you develop the worksheet.

With the Format command make the first five rows, columns 1 through 5, continuous. Type the titles **RETIREMENT LAND** and **BEGINNING BALANCE** in cells R1C2 and R4C1. Move the cell pointer to R4C3 and with the FORMAT cells command enter a **$** in the "format code:" field, press ENTER to set the format, and then type the value **25000** in that cell. Type **4/1/83** as text at R4C5.

Move the cell pointer to row 6 and type the column headings. Move the cell pointer to R6C2 and with the FORMAT cells command center the column headings for columns 2 through 5. To do this, use the following command line:

FORMAT cells: R6C2:5   alignment: Def(Ctr)Gen Left Right
format code:(Def)Cont Exp Fix Gen Int $ * %—   # of decimals: 0

Next move the cell pointer to R7C1 to enter the separator between the headings and the data. Press ENTER to select the Alpha command; then type ten = marks and press ENTER. Use the Copy command to copy this entry to the next four columns.

Enter abbreviations for the months April through December in column 1, rows 8 through 16.

Now use the Name command to name the headings in columns 2 through 5 and the BEGINNING BALANCE title at R4C1. You will use these names to build your formulas. Each name will refer to the data in rows 8 through 16 in its column; cell R4C3 will refer to the BEGINNING BALANCE. In each case you'll use the column heading as the name.

Move the cell pointer to R6C2 and press Name. By default, PAYMENT is suggested for the name, so press the TAB key to move to the "to refer to:" field and type **R8C2:R16C2**. Your command line looks like this:

NAME: define name: PAYMENT   to refer to:R16C2:R16C2

Press ENTER. Use the column headings INTEREST, PRINCIPAL, and BALANCE for the names of the remaining columns. Your default response in the "to refer to:" field will be correct, so merely move the cell pointer over each of these headings, press Name, and press ENTER. The column heading BEGINNING BALANCE will be displayed with an underscore character in place of the space; Multiplan does this automatically and you can ignore it. Type **R4C3** in the "to refer to:" field for this name.

Using the Format command, set up the worksheet area R8C2:R16C5 to present data to two decimal places. You can format the entire area in one operation. Move the cell pointer to R8C2 and press Format and ENTER to select the Cells subcommand. R8C2 is displayed in the "cells:" field, so type a colon (the range operator) and press the END key to move to R16C5. Press the TAB key to move to the "alignment:" field and then press Ctr. Move the edit cursor to the "format code:" field and press Fix. Again press the TAB key to move to the "# of decimals:" field, and type **2**. Before you press ENTER, compare your command line with the following:

FORMAT cells: R8C2:R16C5   alignment: Def(Ctr)Gen Left Right
format code: Def Cont Exp(Fix)Gen Int $ * % —   # of decimals:2

Press ENTER.

You are now ready to enter the worksheet values and formulas. Move the cell pointer to R8C2. The monthly payment is $350, so type in **350**. Use the Copy command to copy this value into the remaining rows of column 2 through row 16. Move the cell pointer to R8C3 and press **V**alue. To enter names in the formula, press F3 and the right arrow until BEGINNING BALANCE appears in the command line. Type a times sign (*), the interest rate, **.11**, and **/12**. Press ENTER.

Move the cell pointer to R8C4 and press **V**alue. Using name references, again enter the formula PAYMENT − INTEREST. Move to R8C5 and enter the formula BEGINNING BALANCE − PRINCIPAL to determine the balance. Move the cell pointer to R9C3 and enter R[−1]C[+2]*.11/12. (Remember to enter the relative reference by moving the cell pointer to the correct cell with the arrow keys.) Move the pointer to R9C5 and enter the formula R[−1]C−PRIN-CIPAL. Then copy the formulas of each column to the last row of the worksheet, row 16. As the formulas are copied into each column, the results are calculated and displayed on the screen. The completed worksheet is shown in Figure 5-2.

One comment on the loan worksheet: Note that 350 was entered in R8C2 and copied to the remaining rows of the column. Entering data in this instance is

```
             1         2         3         4         5
        1              RETIREMENT LAND
        2
        3
        4  BEGINNING BALANCE    $25000.00              4/1/83
        5
        6  MONTH       PAYMENT    INTEREST PRINCIPAL  BALANCE
        7  =====================================================
        8  APRIL        350.00     229.17    120.83   24879.17
        9  MAY          350.00     228.06    121.94   24757.23
       10  JUNE         350.00     226.94    123.06   24634.17
       11  JULY         350.00     225.81    124.19   24509.98
       12  AUGUST       350.00     224.67    125.33   24384.65
       13  SEPT         350.00     223.53    126.47   24258.18
       14  OCT          350.00     222.37    127.63   24130.55
       15  NOV          350.00     221.20    128.80   24001.74
       16  DEC          350.00     220.02    129.98   23871.76
       17
       18
       19
```

Figure 5-2. *RETIREMENT LAND worksheet*

satisfactory, because the value will not change unless the loan is renegotiated. In general, though, it is better to use formulas so you can change the data for an entire column with a single entry. In this case, if R8C2 contained 350 and R9C2 contained R[−1]C and was copied to the remaining rows, a change in R8C2 would affect the entire column.

Using the Print Command

It is very simple to print worksheets with the Print command, assuming your printer is set up properly. Before you begin, turn your printer on and check the paper supply.

Print/Printer

Press **P**rinter and you see the following command line:

PRINT: <u>Printer</u> File Margins Options

Press ENTER to select the Printer subcommand. The RETIREMENT LAND worksheet, which is currently in the computer's memory, should be printed as shown in Figure 5-3. While your worksheet is printing, you may notice an error that slipped by your careful proofreading prior to the printing. You may interrupt the printing at any time by pressing the ESC key. Return to the worksheet, make the necessary changes, and begin the print procedure again.

When the print process is allowed to run its course, the complete worksheet is printed, but its placement on the paper is determined by Multiplan's default options. Let's examine the PRINT subcommands that allow you to modify these options.

Print/Margins

Press **P**rint and **M**argins and you see the following command line:

PRINT MARGINS: left: 5   top: 6   print width: 70
print length: 54   page length: 66

The values shown in each field are the default values, which are set for standard 8 1/2-by-11-inch paper. By entering the appropriate values in the fields, you can determine where on the paper the worksheet will be printed. You may want to change some or all of these default values. When you print the RETIREMENT LAND worksheet again, you'll come back to this command line and set the appropriate values for the worksheet.

```
        RETIREMENT LAND

BEGINNING BALANCE    $25000.00            4/1/83

MONTH       PAYMENT    INTEREST PRINCIPAL   BALANCE
=================================================
APRIL       350.00     229.17    120.83    24879.17
MAY         350.00     228.06    121.94    24757.23
JUNE        350.00     226.94    123.06    24634.17
JULY        350.00     225.81    124.19    24509.98
AUGUST      350.00     224.67    125.33    24384.65
SEPT        350.00     223.53    126.47    24258.18
OCT         350.00     222.37    127.63    24130.55
NOV         350.00     221.20    128.80    24001.74
DEC         350.00     220.02    129.98    23871.76
```

Figure 5-3.   *Printed RETIREMENT LAND worksheet*

When you save a worksheet, whatever PRINT MARGINS values have been set are saved with the worksheet and will be used again the next time the worksheet is loaded. This is also true of the next command, PRINT OPTIONS. Now press ENTER to return to the PRINT command menu.

Print/Options

Press **O**ptions and you get this command line:

```
PRINT OPTIONS: area:R1:255        setup:
formulas: Yes(No)        row-col numbers: Yes(No)
```

Again Multiplan's default values are displayed. The "area:" field allows you to specify the area of the worksheet that you wish to print. The default value R1:255 prints all rows or the entire worksheet area. The "setup:" field allows you to control certain printer functions. Because of the large variety of printers in use, the options for this field will not be discussed. You will have to consult the manual for your printer in order to determine what formats your printer is capable of handling. The "formulas:" field gives you the option of printing the formulas or their results. The default format shown in Figure 5-3 prints the results in each cell rather than the formulas. The final field, "row-col numbers:", gives you the option of choosing whether or not to print the row and column numbers that are always displayed on the screen. Press ENTER now to return to the PRINT command menu.

Printing a File

You're ready to adjust the PRINT OPTIONS and PRINT MARGINS for the RETIREMENT PLAN worksheet. From the PRINT menu select **O**ptions. In the "area:" field type the worksheet block range, **R1C1:R16C5**. In the "formulas:" field leave NO in parentheses because the formulas will not be printed. The same is true of the "row-col numbers:" field because these will not be printed either. Press ENTER when your command line looks like this:

```
PRINT OPTIONS: area:R1C1:R16C5        setup:
formulas: Yes(No)        row-col numbers: Yes(No)
```

You have returned to the PRINT menu with the edit cursor over Printer.

Because the worksheet is narrow, it will not be properly centered on the page from left to right. You can easily correct the problem. From the PRINT menu press **M**argins. You didn't change the width of any of the columns when you entered this worksheet, so the worksheet is 50 characters wide — 5 columns by 10 characters per column.

If you are printing in 10 pitch, that is, 10 characters per inch, you can print 85 columns on paper 8 1/2 inches wide. You therefore have 35 blank columns (85−50=35). To center the worksheet on the page, you have to put half the blank columns at the left margin, so in the "left:" field type **17**. Because you usually don't worry about centering from top to bottom when printing a worksheet, the remaining field entries are satisfactory. The command line displays the following:

PRINT MARGINS: left: 17   top: 6   print width: 70
print length: 54   page length: 66

Press ENTER to return to the PRINT command.

Again the edit cursor is over the Printer subcommand, so press ENTER to print the worksheet. Your hard copy is printed with the worksheet centered on the page.

Printing Formulas

Multiplan allows you to print a worksheet in which each cell shows the formulas you have entered rather than the values calculated. This is useful when you need to proofread your worksheet entries for possible errors. Normally when you print formulas, you also print the Multiplan row and column numbers, so you can easily see where each entry is located on the worksheet.

To print a worksheet with formulas, first select the PRINT OPTIONS command. In the "formulas:" field and in the "row-col numbers:" field use the space bar to enter Yes. Press ENTER to return to the Print command.

When you print formulas, the column widths assigned to that worksheet automatically double. Press **M**argins and change the left margin to 3, since it is still set to 17 from your last entry. In this example, the output will be 100 columns wide, which is wider than the paper. Multiplan will print within the margins set and print the remaining columns on successive sheets of paper. Two sheets of paper will be required to print the formulas in your sample worksheet. Press ENTER to return to the PRINT menu; press it again to select the Printer subcommand and to start printing. You should have two pages of output as shown in Figure 5-4. Look at the figure. On the formula worksheet, text entries are enclosed in quotation marks, while the names used in formulas are not. Also note that in row 8 the formulas for interest and balance did not fit in the double

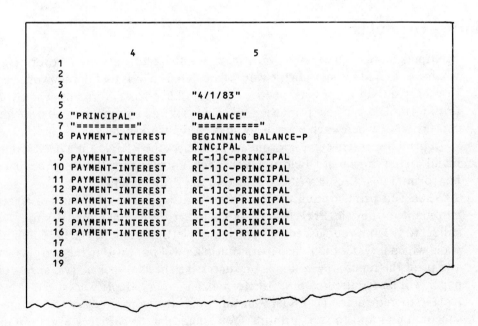

```
 1                  2                3
 1                        "RETIREMENT LAND"
 2
 3
 4 "BEGINNING BALANCE"                   25000
 5
 6 "MONTH"          "PAYMENT"        "INTEREST"
 7 "=========="     "=========="     "=========="
 8 "APRIL"          350              BEGINNING_BALANCE*0
                                     .11/12
 9 "MAY"            350              R[-1]C[+2]*0.11/12
10 "JUNE"           350              R[-1]C[+2]*0.11/12
11 "JULY"           350              R[-1]C[+2]*0.11/12
12 "AUGUST"         350              R[-1]C[+2]*0.11/12
13 "SEPT"           350              R[-1]C[+2]*0.11/12
14 "OCT"            350              R[-1]C[+2]*0.11/12
15 "NOV"            350              R[-1]C[+2]*0.11/12
16 "DEC"            350              R[-1]C[+2]*0.11/12
17
18
19
```

```
                  4                5
 1
 2
 3
 4                        "4/1/83"
 5
 6 "PRINCIPAL"      "BALANCE"
 7 "=========="     "=========="
 8 PAYMENT-INTEREST BEGINNING_BALANCE-P
                    RINCIPAL
 9 PAYMENT-INTEREST R[-1]C-PRINCIPAL
10 PAYMENT-INTEREST R[-1]C-PRINCIPAL
11 PAYMENT-INTEREST R[-1]C-PRINCIPAL
12 PAYMENT-INTEREST R[-1]C-PRINCIPAL
13 PAYMENT-INTEREST R[-1]C-PRINCIPAL
14 PAYMENT-INTEREST R[-1]C-PRINCIPAL
15 PAYMENT-INTEREST R[-1]C-PRINCIPAL
16 PAYMENT-INTEREST R[-1]C-PRINCIPAL
17
18
19
```

Figure 5-4. *Printed formulas for the RETIREMENT LAND worksheet*

column width set by Multiplan and were therefore printed on two lines. You have no control over this width, but you can shorten the names assigned to the data. For example, instead of using the full name BEGINNING BALANCE you could have used BEGBAL. It is worthwhile to keep the names descriptive, but it is also useful to have the formulas print on a single line so they are easier to read.

Since printing formulas automatically doubles the column width, it is normally better to print formulas on wider paper. If you have this option, load your printer with 13 1/2-by-11-inch paper. Remember, of course, to use the Margin command to adjust the "left:" and "paper width:" fields to appropriate values.

Exercises

1. Print the TIMES TABLE worksheet of Chapter 4 with row and column numbers.

2. Print the TIMES TABLE worksheet again, but this time center the output from left to right and from top to bottom. Do not print the row and column numbers.

3. Print the table again, but this time print the formulas.

Reorganizing
Your Worksheet

- Moving Rows and Columns
- Inserting Rows and Columns
- Test Scores
- Changing the Worksheet
- Using the Help File

Commands

- MOVE ROW
- MOVE COLUMN
- INSERT ROW
- INSERT COLUMN
- Help

When you add data to a worksheet, you may sometimes have to rearrange the data already entered. There can be many reasons for this. Perhaps you have discovered a more efficient plan or have obtained new information that needs to be incorporated into the worksheet. You already know some commands — Copy, Blank, and Delete — that help you reorganize a worksheet. In this chapter you will become familiar with two new and powerful commands for this purpose: Move and Insert. In addition, you will see how to use the Help file to review information about commands.

Moving Rows and Columns

To learn the technique of moving rows and columns of data, you will want to use a very simple worksheet. Starting with a clean worksheet, type the letters **A** through **E** in the first five rows of column 1. Your screen should look like this:

```
        1          2          3
  1 A
  2 B
  3 C
  4 D
  5 E
```

Move/Row

First you'll move the letter A and place it between the letters C and D. With the cell pointer in R1C1, press **M**ove and the command line displays

MOVE <u>Row</u> Column

Since you are going to move a row and the Row option is highlighted, press ENTER. Your command line displays

MOVE ROW from row: 1   to before row: 1   # of rows: 1

As with many of Multiplan's commands, the values displayed in the command-line fields record the position of the cell pointer when the command was entered. For your move, change the value in the "to before row:" field to 4:

MOVE ROW from row: 1   to before row: 4   # of rows: 1

Now let's interpret what the command line is telling you. You're going to take the content of row 1 and move it *before* row 4, and you're going to move only one row (that is, "# of rows:" specifies the number of rows of data that are to be moved, not the distance to be moved). Now press ENTER. The letter A should move on your worksheet as shown below, from row 1 to row 3, just above D:

```
        1          2          3
  1 B
  2 C
  3 A
  4 D
  5 E
```

Notice that since the letter A was moved out of row 1, the letters below it moved up to occupy rows 1 and 2.

Multiplan does not limit you to moving a single row at a time. To see how it's done, this time you'll move two rows. Again with the cell pointer in the home position press **M**ove and then ENTER to select the Row option. Change your command line now so that it reads

MOVE ROW from row: 1   to before row: 4   # of rows: 2

You're instructing Multiplan to take two rows of data starting at row 1 and move them before row 4. Press ENTER to execute this command. Your screen should look like this:

```
              1              2              3
1  A
2  B
3  C
4  D
5  E
```

The letters are back in alphabetical order.

You can also move rows to areas that contain no data. To see how, place the cell pointer in R2C1. Select the MOVE ROW command by pressing **M**ove and ENTER. Enter the data in the fields as indicated here:

MOVE ROW from row: 2   to before row: 9   # of rows: 3

Press ENTER. The text is moved as shown:

```
              1              2              3
 1  A
 2  E
 3
 4
 5
 6  B
 7  C
 8  D
 9
10
```

Not only did rows 2 through 4 move as indicated in the command line, but when they did so the letter E moved up from row 5 to close up the empty space.

Move/Column

Now let's move columns of data in the worksheet. Use TRANSFER CLEAR to blank your worksheet and the FORMAT WIDTH command to change the widths of columns 1 through 10 to 3. Next use the FORMAT cells command to format these columns so that the data entered will be centered (and your screen will match the samples shown in the book). Type the letters **A** through **E** in columns 1 through 5 as shown:

```
    1  2  3  4  5  6  7  8  9  10
1   A  B  C  D  E
2
```

With your cell pointer in the home position, press **M**ove and **C**olumn. Your command line displays the following:

MOVE COLUMN from column: 1 to left of column: 1 # of columns: 1

Just as the Row command moves whole rows, the Column command moves whole columns. As an example, change the 1 to a 4 in the second field of the command line, "to left of column:":

MOVE COLUMN from column: 1 to left of column: 4 # of columns: 1

The command line is now instructing Multiplan to move the contents of column 1 to the left of column 4, and to move just one column. Press ENTER and your screen should look like this:

```
    1  2  3  4  5  6  7  8  9  10
1   B  C  A  D  E
2
```

You can also move more than one column at a time. To see how, place the cell pointer in R1C4 and press **M**ove and **C**olumn. Change the third field value, "# of columns:", from 1 to 2:

MOVE COLUMN from column: 4 to left of column: 1 # of columns: 2

The command line is telling Multiplan to move the contents of column 4 to the left of column 1, that is, to move two columns, columns 4 and 5. Press ENTER and the display is rearranged as follows:

```
    1  2  3  4  5  6  7  8  9  10
1   D  E  B  C  A
2
```

As a final example, let's move the contents of columns 2, 3, and 4 so they occupy columns 7, 8, and 9. Press **M**ove and **C**olumn and change the data in the command fields as follows:

MOVE COLUMN from column: 2 to left of column: 10 # of columns: 3

Examine the command line and the values in each field to be sure you are making the desired move. Press ENTER and your screen display appears as shown.

```
    1  2  3  4  5  6  7  8  9  10
 1  D  A              E  B  C
 2
```

Notice that the A in column 5 moved to the left and now occupies column 2. Data in column 10 and beyond would not move left or right.

Inserting Rows and Columns

Another command that is very helpful in reorganizing a worksheet is the Insert command. With this command you can insert blank rows and columns into a worksheet. The rows and columns you insert can be partial or complete.

So that your screens will match the displays shown in the discussion that follows, perform these steps: Blank your screen and use the FORMAT WIDTH command to change the widths of columns 1 through 10 to 3; use the FORMAT cells command to center data in R1C1:R10C10.

Now enter the data shown in the next example. First type the letters **A, C, E,**

G, and **I** in column 1; then use the Copy command to copy the data in column 1 into the next four columns.

```
    1  2  3  4  5  6  7  8  9 10
1   A  A  A  A  A
2   C  C  C  C  C
3   E  E  E  E  E
4   G  G  G  G  G
5   I  I  I  I  I
```

Insert/Row

With the cell pointer in the home position, press **I**nsert and the command line displays the following:

   INSERT: Row Column

Let's insert rows first. Since the Row subcommand is highlighted, press ENTER. You now have the following command line:

   INSERT ROW # of rows: 1   before row: 1
   between columns: 1   and: 63

First you will insert a row between the row of A's and the row of C's in the worksheet. Change the value in field 2 so the command line reads

   INSERT ROW # of row: 1   before row: 2
   between columns: 1   and: 63

Press ENTER. A blank line has been inserted at row 2, and the data previously contained in rows 2 through 5 has moved down one row:

```
    1  2  3  4  5  6  7  8  9 10
1   A  A  A  A  A
2
3   C  C  C  C  C
4   E  E  E  E  E
5   G  G  G  G  G
6   I  I  I  I  I
```

Now move the cell pointer to R2C1 and type the letter **B** into this cell. Your screen should look like this:

```
    1  2  3  4  5  6  7  8  9 10
1   A  A  A  A  A
2   B
3   C  C  C  C  C
4   E  E  E  E  E
5   G  G  G  G  G
6   I  I  I  I  I
```

Notice that when you inserted the row your column widths did not change, but the new row does not center data as you previously formatted the worksheet area. An entire row or column that is inserted into a worksheet has the default format, and so you must reformat the new row 2 to center data. Do this now and then use the Copy command to insert the letter B in column 1 into the next four columns:

```
   1  2  3  4  5  6  7  8  9 10
1  A  A  A  A  A
2  B  B  B  B  B
3  C  C  C  C  C
4  E  E  E  E  E
5  G  G  G  G  G
6  I  I  I  I  I
```

The next example illustrates two operations: first, inserting more than one row at a time; second, inserting a portion of a row. To begin, press Insert and ENTER to select the Row subcommand. Next change the field values in the INSERT ROW command line to match these:

INSERT ROW # of rows: 2   before row: 3
between columns: 2   and: 4

You are going to insert two rows, but as the third and fourth field values show, the rows are only three columns in length.

Press ENTER and your screen looks like this:

```
   1  2  3  4  5  6  7  8  9 10
1  A  A  A  A  A
2  B  B  B  B  B
3  C           C
4  E           E
5  G  C  C  C  G
6  I  E  E  E  I
7     G  G  G
8     I  I  I
```

There are two points you should note about this display. First, although the newly inserted blank area R3C2:R4C4 falls within an area that was formatted to center data, the new cells are not so formatted. Data entered in these cells will not be centered unless you now format the cells. Second, note that the data in R7C2 through R8C4, which was moved down when the partial rows were inserted above them, remains centered as formatted.

Before going on to the next section, use the Delete command to delete this blank section in the center of your data. You should again have a solid block of data on your worksheet.

Insert/Column

To see how to insert columns, move the cell pointer to R1C4, then press **I**nsert and **C**olumn. Your command line displays

> INSERT COLUMN # of columns: 1   before column: 4
> between rows: 1   and: 255

Change the values in the first field to match the following display:

> INSERT COLUMN # of columns: 3   before column: 4
> between rows: 1   and: 255

The command line is similar to that of the INSERT ROW command. Here Multiplan is instructed to insert three columns before column 4. Press ENTER and the screen should look like this:

```
   1  2  3     4         5         6     7  8  9 10 11 12 13
1  A  A  A                             A  A
2  B  B  B                             B  B
3  C  C  C                             C  C
4  E  E  E                             E  E
5  G  G  G                             G  G
6  I  I  I                             I  I
```

Notice that the inserted columns 4, 5, and 6 have the default width of 10 characters. Also notice that columns 11, 12, and 13 have the width 3, although only columns 1 through 10 were so formatted earlier. When you inserted the three columns, the previous columns 4 through 10 were moved to columns 7 through 13, and all the columns retained the previous column width of 3.

Now use the FORMAT WIDTH and FORMAT cells commands to set the width and to center the data entered in columns 4, 5, and 6. Type an **X** in R1C4 and copy it to the block R1C4:R6C6. Your screen displays the following:

```
   1  2  3  4  5  6  7  8  9 10 11 12 13
1  A  A  A  X  X  X  A  A
2  B  B  B  X  X  X  B  B
3  C  C  C  X  X  X  C  C
4  E  E  E  X  X  X  E  E
5  G  G  G  X  X  X  G  G
6  I  I  I  X  X  X  I  I
```

Now let's insert partial columns—two columns between rows 2 and 5. Press **I**nsert and **C**olumn. Change your field entries to match the following command line:

> INSERT COLUMN # of columns: 2   before column: 4
> between rows: 2   and: 5

Here you've instructed Multiplan to insert two columns the length of rows 2 through 5 before column 4. Press ENTER and your screen should be rearranged as follows:

```
   1  2  3  4  5  6  7  8  9 10
1  A  A  A  X  X  X  A  A
2  B  B  B        X  X  X  B  B
3  C  C  C        X  X  X  C  C
4  E  E  E        X  X  X  E  E
5  G  G  G        X  X  X  G  G
6  I  I  I  X  X  X  I  I
```

A few last words about the Insert command. You cannot insert rows or columns into a worksheet if it would cause data to be pushed off the edge or the bottom of the worksheet. For example, if you had data in column 63, you could not insert another column in the worksheet even if there were blank columns. Also, any time an entire row or column is inserted in the worksheet, it assumes the default format even if it is inserted in the middle of a preformatted section of the sheet. Changing the default format will be discussed in Chapter 7.

The Move and Insert commands, along with Copy, Delete, and Blank, give you a great deal of flexibility in rearranging any worksheet.

Test Scores

To become more practiced in using these new commands, try developing a worksheet to keep track of students' test scores in a physics class.

The planning sheet for the worksheet is shown in Figure 6-1. The parentheses above each column number indicate the column width (the d stands for the default width, 10). Reading down the right column, notice that row 2, columns 2 through 5, is formatted as continuous, and that in row 4 the titles enclosed in parentheses are right-justified. The underlined titles are to be used as Name references. (The titles used are descriptive, so use them for the names you assign.) The portion of the worksheet to which each name applies is listed at the bottom of the worksheet.

After formatting the worksheet appropriately, enter the data supplied in Table 6-1. Your worksheet should look like the screen shown in Figure 6-2.

Changing the Worksheet

Now suppose that after entering the data you decide to make some changes. First try inserting more information at the beginning of the sheet. Move the cell pointer to R3C1 and use the Insert command to insert two rows before row 3.

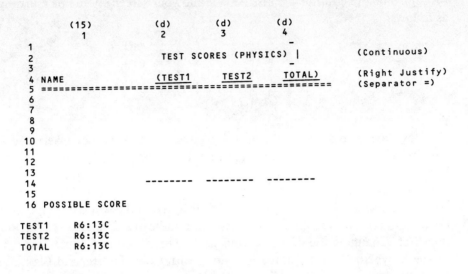

```
        (15)          (d)       (d)       (d)
         1             2         3         4
                                           -
 1
 2                        TEST SCORES (PHYSICS) |            (Continuous)
 3                                         -
 4 NAME                (TEST1     TEST2     TOTAL)           (Right Justify)
 5 =========================================================            (Separator =)
 6
 7
 8
 9
10
11
12
13
14                    --------  --------  --------
15
16 POSSIBLE SCORE

   TEST1    R6:13C
   TEST2    R6:13C
   TOTAL    R6:13C
```

Figure 6-1. *Planning sheet for TEST SCORES worksheet*

```
                 1          2        3        4
 1
 2                    TEST SCORES (PHYSICS)
 3
 4 NAME                TEST1     TEST2     TOTAL
 5 =========================================================
 6 ADAMS                 54        30
 7 ANSEL                 61        31
 8 CAMPBELL              60        29
 9 COPPER                49        25
10 DUNN                  33        21
11 ETTENGER              52        23
12 MCMURRY               53        29
13 SHAW                  44        27
14                    --------  --------  --------
15
16 POSSIBLE SCORE        65        33
```

Figure 6-2. *The formatted worksheet with data entered*

Name	Test 1	Test 2
ADAMS	54	30
ANSEL	61	31
CAMPBELL	60	29
COPPER	49	25
DUNN	33	21
ETTENGER	52	23
MCMURRY	53	29
SHAW	44	27
POSSIBLE SCORE	65	33

Table 6-1. *Test Score Data*

Format these two rows to be continuous through column 5, and type the heading **SECOND PERIOD** in row 3 and the heading **FIRST SEMESTER '83** in row 4. The heading of your worksheet should now look like this:

```
                1              2           3           4
   1
   2                       TEST SCORES (PHYSICS)
   3                          SECOND PERIOD
   4                        FIRST SEMESTER '83
   5
```

For a second change, let's suppose that a new student, named Jamieson, enters the class. Move your cell pointer to R13C1 and again press Insert, ENTER for Row, and ENTER again to insert the new row. Now type the new name, **JAMIESON,** and two test scores, **59** and **28.**

Third let's suppose that one of the young ladies in the class, Ms. Campbell, got married and changed her name to Radder. Place the cell pointer over CAMP-BELL, and with the Alpha command, change the name by typing **RADDER.** Press ENTER to enter the name. Then, to realphabetize the list, use the Move command to place RADDER between MCMURRY and SHAW. Press **M**ove and ENTER for Row, change the value in the "to before row:" field to **16,** and press ENTER. Your worksheet is again in alphabetical order.

Finally, suppose you wish to add a column to your worksheet to include a TEST3. Move the cell pointer to column 4 (it can be in any row), and press Insert and **C**olumn. The command line displays the correct values in each field, so press ENTER.

Type the title **TEST3** in row 6 at column 4. Right-justify this title using the FORMAT cells command. In R7C4 enter the separator, the equal marks that separate the titles from the data, and finally, in R17C4, copy the dashes from R17C3. Use TEST3 as a Name reference for the column of data in R8:16 below it. Your worksheet should look like the screen shown in Figure 6-3.

One important item to note is that the Name references have automatically adjusted to include the new row of data that was inserted. Thus, TEST1, for example, still names all of the TEST1 scores.

In Chapter 7 you are going to add much more to this worksheet, so save it under the name PHY.C6. When you return to it, you will be determining student totals and other test data, to become adept in using mathematical operators and functions.

Using the Help File

You've seen that the Multiplan message line prompts you in the use of various program commands and subcommands. Another aid that Multiplan provides is called the *Help file*.

If you usually remove the Multiplan disk for safety reasons after the program has been loaded, then you cannot use the Help file unless you have already

```
                 1            2          3        4          5
   1
   2                     TEST SCORES (PHYSICS)
   3                       SECOND PERIOD
   4                     FIRST SEMESTER '83
   5
   6  NAME               TEST1      TEST2    TEST3      TOTAL
   7  ========================================================
   8  ADAMS                54         30
   9  ANSEL                61         31
  10  COPPER               49         25
  11  DUNN                 33         21
  12  ETTENGER             52         23
  13  JAMIESON             59         28
  14  MCMURRY              53         29
  15  RADDER               60         29
  16  SHAW                 44         27
  17                    --------   --------  --------   --------
  18
  19  POSSIBLE SCORE       65         33
```

Figure 6-3. *The worksheet after use of Insert and Move commands*

loaded it on your data disk. Look in your data disk directory for the filename MP.HLP. If it is not there, copy the file from your Multiplan disk to your data disk. Load Multiplan into the computer. Now you'll examine the ways to make use of the Help file. First, while the command menu is displayed, press **Help**. The first page of the Help file is displayed on the screen, and the Help subcommand line is displayed as follows:

> HELP: <u>Resume</u> Start Next Previous
> Applications Commands Editing Formulas Keyboard

You choose a command from this menu just as you do from the menus you have already worked with. Press F10 or the space bar to move the edit cursor forward through the list, press F9 or BACKSPACE to move it backward through the list, and then press ENTER when the desired command is highlighted. You may choose any subcommand simply by pressing the first letter of its name. The commands on the first line are as follows:

Resume	Returns you to the worksheet. (You can also press ESC.)
Start	Returns you from any point in the Help file to the beginning of the file.
Next	Displays the next page of the Help file. (You can also use the PGDN key.)
Previous	Displays the previous page in the Help file. (You can also use the PGUP key.)

The second line of Help subcommands enables you to select short Help file tutorials on the various topics listed. You can select any of these for a quick review of Multiplan instructions. It would be worth your time now to try each of the subcommands in the Help menu to see how the Help file functions and to acquaint yourself with the type of help available there.

Now return to the worksheet: if the edit cursor is over Resume, press ENTER; or press **R**esume or the ESC key to cancel the command.

A Help file tutorial is also available for every command on the main command menu — Alpha, Blank, Copy, and so on. You can get this help after you have selected a command from the main menu. For example, press Format to display the Format subcommand options. But suppose you forget how to use the Format command. Press ALT and **H**elp simultaneously, and Multiplan branches off to the section of the Help file that explains the Format command.

The tutorials of many commands are more than one screen of text. The Format tutorial, for example, consists of seven screens. To read all seven, press **N**ext to move down a page or **P**revious to move back a page. You can also use the

PGDN and PGUP keys to move to the next or previous screen.

There are two ways to return to the worksheet after selecting **H**elp from the command file. Pressing ENTER with the edit cursor over Resume returns you to the worksheet and the same command submenu (Format, for example) that was on display when you selected Help. Pressing ESC returns you to the worksheet and the main command line.

Familiarize yourself with what is available from the Help file by using both methods of Help file selection.

Exercises

To gain experience with Move and Insert, try the following exercises.

Note: If you wish to save the worksheets with the changes you make in these exercises, use filenames other than the current ones. In that way, when you add to the originals in later chapters, their data and format will be the same as shown in the book.

1. Load the NATIONAL LEAGUE worksheet you constructed in Chapter 2. Delete the Pct. and GB columns, and use the Move command to rearrange the teams so they are in alphabetical order.

2. In the TEST SCORES worksheet add the following names and test data in the appropriate rows:
   Lyons   63, 32
   Harris   57, 27
   Sharp   49, 29

3. In the TEST SCORES worksheet add a column before Test1, and title the column HOMEWORK. Assign HOMEWORK as the Name reference for the column, complete the separator in row 7, add the dashes at the bottom of the column, and right-justify the title.

Formatting, Mathematical Operators, and Functions

- Working With Mathematical Operators
- Using Format/Default
- Rounding Numbers for Display
- Working With Functions
- Test Scores
- Using a Dummy Column or Row
- Using Edit
- Locking and Unlocking Cells and Formulas
- Displaying Formulas in a Worksheet

Commands

- FORMAT DEFAULT
- Edit
- LOCK cells
- LOCK FORMULAS
- FORMAT OPTIONS

Functions

- SUM
- AVERAGE
- COUNT

In the worksheets you have developed so far, any mathematical formulas you needed were supplied. In this chapter you will learn about the mathematical operators you need in order to develop your own formulas. The chapter also includes more detailed information on formatting and introduces three of Multiplan's most commonly used mathematical functions. In short, this chapter will help you build your own formulas.

Working With Mathematical Operators

Most of the practical purposes for which you use worksheets require that you use mathematical formulas, which in turn require *mathematical operators,* the symbols that cause mathematical operations to be performed. The operators available with Multiplan are percentage (%), exponentiation (^), multiplication (*), division (/), addition (+), and subtraction (−).

Order of Precedence

In any formula containing more than one mathematical operator, no two operators can be executed at the same time. They must be done in a sequence, and the sequence can determine the outcome: for example, $4 + 1 \times 2$ can equal either 6 (if you add 4 to 1 multiplied by 2) or 10 (if you multiply the sum of 4 and 1 by 2). To obtain the correct results when using mathematical operators in a complicated formula, you must understand their *order of precedence,* the order in which mathematical operations take place. The order of precedence is shown in Table 7-1. Multiplication and division have the same order of precedence, as do addition and subtraction. Operations having the same order of precedence are calculated as they occur in a formula from left to right.

Here are some simple formulas in which mathematical operators are combined.

$$4 + 3 - 2 = 5$$

Addition and subtraction are of the same order. They therefore are executed in the order in which they occur from left to right.

$$3 + 6/3 = 5$$

Division is of a higher order than addition. Multiplan first divides 6 by 3 and then adds the result, 2, to 3.

$$5 - 3^\wedge 2 = -4$$

Exponentiation (the multiplying of a number by itself a given number of times) is of a higher order than subtraction, so 3 is first squared to give 9, and 9 is subtracted from 5.

$$4 * 3^\wedge 2 = 36$$

Operator	Operation	Order
%	Percent	Highest
^	Exponentiation	
*,/	Multiplication, division	
+,−	Addition, subtraction	Lowest

Table 7-1.   *Mathematical Operators*

Exponentiation takes precedence over multiplication, so 3 is first squared to give 9, and then 9 is multiplied by 4.

$6/2^{\wedge}3 = 0.75$

Exponentiation is calculated before division, so 2 is first cubed to give 8, and then 8 is divided into 6 to give the result, 0.75.

$15\% * 50 = 7.5$

Since percent is highest in the order of precedence, the 15 is first converted to 0.15 and then multiplied by 50 to give the result, 7.5.

To verify the results, blank the worksheet and type the left expression of each formula (everything to the left of the equals sign) into a cell and press ENTER.

Changing the Order of Precedence With Parentheses

You can control the order in which operations take place by using parentheses. An operation contained in parentheses is performed before any other. Here are a few examples of how parentheses are used to control the order of precedence and thereby affect the result of a formula.

$(3 + 6)/3 = 3$

Because the operation $3 + 6$ is enclosed in parentheses, addition is performed first, even though division has a higher order of precedence. After the 3 and 6 are added, the result is divided by 3 to give the final result, 3.

$2 * (5 + 6) = 22$

Even though the multiplication operator occurs first when the formula is read from left to right, and multiplication is higher in order of precedence than addition, addition is performed first because the operation is enclosed in parentheses, and the result is then multiplied by 2.

$(5 - 2)^{\wedge}2 = 9$

Because of the parentheses, 2 is subtracted from 5 and the result, 3, is raised to the second power to give the final result, 9.

$((4 + 2) * 3)/2 = 9$

When one set of parentheses is enclosed, or "nested," in another set, as in this example, the operations in the innermost parentheses are executed first. Therefore $4 + 2$ is calculated to give the result 6, which is then multiplied by 3 (to conclude the second parenthetical operation), and finally that result, 18, is divided by 2 to give the answer, 9. When you "nest" sets of parentheses like this, be sure that you have an equal number of left and right parentheses, or your formula will produce an error.

$$(4 + 2) * (3 - 1)/4 = 3$$

In this example, Multiplan first evaluates each operation in parentheses: $4 + 2 = 6$ and $3 - 1 = 2$. Multiplication and division, being of equal order of precedence, are executed in order from left to right: 6×2 is 12, which is divided by 4 to give the result, 3.

To verify the results, enter the left expression of each formula into a Multiplan worksheet.

Using Format/Default

Occasionally, when working with Multiplan, you will find it convenient to change the default format settings for the entire worksheet. You can do this by using the FORMAT DEFAULT command. Press **F**ormat and **D**efault, and your command line displays

FORMAT DEFAULT: <u>Cells</u> Width

The values you set for either subcommand option, Cells or Width, apply to all the cells or column widths in the worksheet, not just to individual rows, cells, or blocks, as in the past.

First consider the Cells subcommand. Press ENTER and your command line displays

FORMAT DEFAULT CELLS alignment: Ctr(Gen)Left Right
format code:Cont Exp Fix(Gen)Int $ * %   # of decimals: 0

The three fields displayed here are the same as those displayed with the FORMAT cells command. The only difference is that when you select a format here, it will automatically affect every cell in the worksheet. (Note, however, that even after changing the default format you can format individual cells, columns, and rows to other values or settings by using the FORMAT cells command.)

Changing the cells' default format may be useful, for example, if you want all values entered on a worksheet to display dollar signs. Use the "format code:" field of the FORMAT DEFAULT CELLS command to highlight the $. Or you may want all the numbers in a worksheet to be displayed with a fixed number of decimal places. In this case, highlight Fix, and in the "# of decimals:" field, set the appropriate value.

Press ESC now to return to the full command line, and press Format, then **D**efault, then **W**idth. The command line looks like this:

FORMAT DEFAULT width in chars: <u>10</u>

The number you enter in this field will set the widths of all the columns in the worksheet. This command can be useful when you work with tables. For example, when entering the TIMES TABLE worksheet in Chapter 4, you could have used this command to set all the columns in the worksheet to a width of 6 characters, since that was the only width used. Another example is in the previous chapter, where you experimented with the Insert command. If you had set the default width to 3, the inserted columns would have been entered with this width, rather than a width of 10. Again, you can always adjust the widths of individual columns after changing the worksheet default by using the FORMAT WIDTH command.

In general, the Multiplan default values are appropriate for most worksheets. Only you can tell if changing any of the default values is useful for your worksheet.

Rounding Numbers for Display

When Multiplan prints numbers, whether those that are typed or those that are the result of mathematical calculations, it displays them as accurately as possible within the column width provided. That is, if a number has, say, eight decimal places, but Multiplan has only six places in which to print the decimal, the number will be rounded to six decimal places. Let's work through some examples that illustrate how this works.

On a clean worksheet, set the width of column 2 to 3 characters and column 4 to 5 characters. Then use the FORMAT cells command to right-justify the contents of columns 1, 3, and 5. Next use the *Alpha* command to enter the following data in the first three rows of column 1:

5/8=
5/11=
5*35=

With the Copy command, copy the same text entries into columns 3 and 5. Your screen should look like this:

```
      1       2      3       4     5         6
1     5/8=           5/8=          5/8=
2     5/11=          5/11=         5/11=
3     5*35=          5*35=         5*35=
4
```

Now, using the *Value* command, enter the same three expressions into column 2, excluding the equals signs. As you do, you'll see the results displayed. Next copy the expressions into columns 4 and 6. You will get the various results shown here:

```
      1       2      3       4      5         6
1     5/8=  1       5/8=0.63        5/8=       0.625
2     5/11= 0       5/11=0.45       5/11=0.4545455
3     5*35=###      5*35= 175       5*35=      175
4
```

Because the three result columns have different widths, Multiplan prints the numbers at different levels of accuracy. In R1C2 the result of 5/8 is printed as 1 (the actual result is 0.625). The reason this result was rounded to 1 (and not 0.6, for example) is that Multiplan really has only one space in which to print the number, even with a 3-character column width. When the Value command is used to print a number in any cell, Multiplan always leaves the rightmost space in the column blank; and it always prints a zero before a decimal. Printing the result of 5/8 more accurately would require three spaces; since only two are available in column 2, it rounds the result to 1.

In R1C4 the column width is 5 and Multiplan can print in four spaces, so it prints the result of 5/8 as 0.63, which is much more accurate than the result in column 2. In column 6 there is ample room to print the complete answer to the problem.

In row 2 the results of the calculation 5/11 are similar in format to the results of the previous problem, except that in column 6 the result fills the column completely. Since 5/11 produces a repeating (infinite) decimal, the answer would go on forever.

Multiplan limits the results of calculations to 14 decimal places. To see the result in R2C6 with 14 decimal places, change the width of column 6 to 17: 14 spaces will be used for the decimal, one space for the decimal point, one space for the zero, and one blank space at the end of the number.

In R3C2 you can see what happens when the number is too large to fit the cell: Multiplan fills the cell with number signs (#). Even though the result, 175, contains only three digits, Multiplan requires a space to the right of the last digit and therefore cannot print this number in column 2.

You can see from this exercise that when the results of calculations are printed, you must be sure that the cells containing the results are sufficiently large to be meaningful and to have the degree of accuracy you desire.

Working With Functions

Multiplan, like any spreadsheet program, has the purpose of making it easy for you to manipulate numbers (and, to a limited extent, text). Multiplan provides many aids for manipulating numbers, called *functions*. (A function does a specific task, such as finding the sum of a list of numbers, counting the number of items in a list, or finding the average of a group of numbers.) Forty-two functions are provided in Multiplan. In this chapter you will be introduced to three of them: SUM, AVERAGE, and COUNT.

Some functions are used frequently by everyone who works with Multiplan, and others are used only in specialized applications such as engineering, test analysis, and the like. In this book you will become familiar with the functions commonly used in building practical worksheets, but you will see only short examples of the more specialized ones.

SUM

Consider the function SUM. The format for the function is SUM(List), where List stands for a series of numbers. This series can be a list of individual numbers separated by commas or a series of values contained in a range of cells.

Suppose you wish to place the sum of the numbers 1, 2, 3, and 4 in a cell. You can use the Value command and type **1+2+3+4**. Or you can accomplish this same task with the SUM function. Press Value and then type **SUM(1,2,3,4)**. The command line looks like this:

VALUE: SUM(1,2,3,4)

Press ENTER and the result of the addition appears in the active cell.

This is a simple example, but when the SUM function is used with ranges designated by absolute reference, relative reference, or Name reference, it becomes a very useful and powerful tool. You'll use it in most of the sample worksheets from now on.

AVERAGE

The AVERAGE function — its format is AVERAGE(List) — finds the average of a list of numbers. The AVERAGE function automatically sums the numbers contained in the list and divides the sum by the number of values. For example, entering (34+54+76+23)/4 or AVERAGE(34,54,76,23) into the active cell will produce the same result, 46.75.

Like the SUM function, the list used with this function may contain values identified by absolute reference, relative reference, Name reference, or it may consist of numbers separated by commas.

COUNT

The COUNT function determines how many numbers there are in a list. The format of the function is COUNT(List). Note that it only counts items that contain numbers; it cannot count the items in a list that contain text. As in the SUM and AVERAGE functions, the list may take various forms. For example, COUNT(1,2,3,4) returns 4, and COUNT(R1C1:R1C10) returns 10 if the first 10 rows of column 1 contain numeric entries.

Test Scores

Now you're ready to use functions in a worksheet. Load the TEST SCORES worksheet, PHY.C6, that you started in the last chapter. Enter the following data for TEST3 in column 4:

ADAMS	65
ANSEL	71
COPPER	60
DUNN	49
ETTENGER	66
JAMIESON	61
MCMURRY	57
RADDER	71
SHAW	53
POSSIBLE SCORE	80

Using SUM

With all the test scores entered, you can use the SUM function to total the scores of the three tests for each student. Follow these steps:

1. Move the cell pointer to R8C5, where the first student's total score will be calculated.
2. Press **Value**, the command used to enter functions.
3. Type **SUM** and (.
4. Move the cell pointer one cell to the left, over the TEST3 score.

This is the opening range entry for the list.

5. Type a :, the range operator.
6. Move the cell pointer three columns to the left, over the TEST1 score.

This is the closing range entry for the list.

7. Type a).

The command line now displays the formula SUM(RC[−1]:RC[−3]).

8. Press ENTER.

The total of the first student's three test scores, 149, is calculated and printed.

9. Copy the formula in R8C5 down column 5 through row 16.

The test score totals are calculated for each student.

You now have the total test score for each student in the class. Copy the formula to R19C5 to obtain the TOTAL POSSIBLE SCORE. Your worksheet should look like the one in Figure 7-1.

```
                1            2         3        4         5
    1
    2                  TEST SCORES (PHYSICS)
    3                     SECOND PERIOD
    4                  FIRST SEMESTER '83
    5
    6  NAME                 TEST1     TEST2    TEST3     TOTAL
    7  ================================================================
    8  ADAMS                  54        30       65       149
    9  ANSEL                  61        31       71       163
   10  COPPER                 49        25       60       134
   11  DUNN                   33        21       49       103
   12  ETTENGER               52        23       66       141
   13  JAMIESON               59        28       61       148
   14  MCMURRY                53        29       57       139
   15  RADDER                 60        29       71       160
   16  SHAW                   44        27       53       124
   17                      --------  --------  --------  --------
   18
   19  POSSIBLE SCORE         65        33       80       178
```

Figure 7-1.   *Worksheet with data entered by SUM function*

Using AVERAGE

Now you can determine the average score for each test. The average is the sum of the test scores divided by the number of people who took the test.

Move the cell pointer to R18C1 and press **Insert** to add one row. In R18C1 type **AVERAGE SCORE**. Move the cell pointer to R18C2, which is where you will calculate the average score for TEST1.

There are three different ways to determine the average in this worksheet. You should review all three because the best method for this particular worksheet may not be appropriate for worksheets that you design yourself.

First consider the formula SUM(TEST1)/9. (Note that in this formula the division symbol and the 9 are outside the parentheses. Only the list may be contained in the function's parentheses; no mathematical operations — or operators — can be placed there.) This formula will sum the values associated with the Name reference TEST1 and then divide by 9. It will yield the correct result but has the disadvantage that if students' names and test scores are added or deleted from the list, the divisor 9 will have to be changed to correspond to the correct number of students.

A second formula for calculating averages is SUM(TEST1)/COUNT (TEST1). This formula has the advantage that if the number of students changes, COUNT will automatically correct the divisor. This is a good method of finding averages, but the next formula is simpler and the best one for the TEST SCORES worksheet.

This formula, AVERAGE(TEST1), automatically sums all the test scores in the list and finds the average. In this case, the list contains the Name reference that in turn contains all the values needed in this calculation. The formula continues to give correct results even if students' names are added to or deleted from the list.

Enter the AVERAGE(TEST1) formula in R18C2. Press ENTER to display the correct result. Do the same to determine the averages of TEST2, TEST3, and TOTAL. Note that you cannot copy the formula from column 2 because in each of these other formulas, the list is different: In column 3 the list is TEST2; in column 4, TEST3; and in column 5, TOTAL.

Now make one more change in row 18. Use the FORMAT cells command to Fix the number of decimals at 2. Your worksheet should look like Figure 7-2.

Now add a column so you can enter data for a fourth test. Move the cell pointer to column 5 and press Insert and Column. The values in each of the fields are correct, so press ENTER. Type the heading **TEST4** in R6C5 and complete the separator line by copying it from column 4 to column 5. Also right-justify the column 5 heading. The worksheet should look like Figure 7-3.

```
              1            2         3        4        5
 1
 2                   TEST SCORES (PHYSICS)
 3                     SECOND PERIOD
 4                   FIRST SEMESTER '83
 5
 6 NAME               TEST1     TEST2    TEST3    TOTAL
 7 ======================================================
 8 ADAMS                 54        30       65      149
 9 ANSEL                 61        31       71      163
10 COPPER                49        25       60      134
11 DUNN                  33        21       49      103
12 ETTENGER              52        23       66      141
13 JAMIESON              59        28       61      148
14 MCMURRY               53        29       57      139
15 RADDER                60        29       71      160
16 SHAW                  44        27       53      124
17                   --------  -------- -------- --------
18 AVERAGE SCORE      51.67     27.00    61.44   140.11
19
20 POSSIBLE SCORE        65        33       80      178
```

Figure 7-2. *Worksheet with data entered by AVERAGE function*

	1	2	3	4	5	6
1						
2		TEST SCORES (PHYSICS)				
3		SECOND PERIOD				
4		FIRST SEMESTER '83				
5						
6	NAME	TEST1	TEST2	TEST3	TEST4	TOTAL
7	===					
8	ADAMS	54	30	65		149
9	ANSEL	61	31	71		163
10	COPPER	49	25	60		134
11	DUNN	33	21	49		103
12	ETTENGER	52	23	66		141
13	JAMIESON	59	28	61		148
14	MCMURRY	53	29	57		139
15	RADDER	60	29	71		160
16	SHAW	44	27	53		124
17		--------	--------	--------		--------
18	AVERAGE SCORE	51.67	27.00	61.44		140.11
19						
20	POSSIBLE SCORE	65	33	80		178

Figure 7-3.   *Worksheet with column inserted*

In cell R8C5, type **51**, the TEST4 score for the first student, and press ENTER. You might have expected that when you pressed ENTER the total for Adams would change. To see why it didn't, move the cell pointer over the 149 in the TOTAL column and notice the formula in the status line at the bottom of the screen. The formula is no longer the one you entered. The relative references, or range *offsets,* −1 and −3 were changed to −2 and −4 when you inserted a column at the boundary of the formula. You could correct the formula now, but this is not the best solution because the same thing will happen again when new test scores are added to the worksheet.

Using a Dummy Column or Row

A better solution is to add a "dummy" column to be used as an outer boundary in the SUM formula. Do this now by inserting a column before column 6. Change the width of this new column to 3 and complete the separator across it.

Move the cell pointer to R8C7. Using relative referencing, enter the formula SUM(RC[−1]:RC[−5]). Press ENTER to display the correct total of the first student's four tests, 200. Since no data is entered in the dummy column, it does not affect the totals. If you add a new column of data to the worksheet, insert it to the left of the dummy column and the formula will automatically include the new data in the TOTAL column.

Enter the following TEST4 scores for the remaining students:

ANSEL   52
COPPER   43
DUNN   43
ETTENGER   47
JAMIESON   57
MCMURRY   42
RADDER   49
SHAW   40

Enter the POSSIBLE SCORE for TEST4 as 55, enter the line at the bottom of the TEST4 scores in row 17, and then enter the formula to determine the AVERAGE SCORE for this test. To finish the calculations, copy the new TOTAL formula down column 7 so that it corrects the total for each student. The totals will automatically be adjusted to include the TEST4 scores. Your worksheet should look like Figure 7-4.

The same difficulty that occurs if you add a column at the boundary of a formula will also occur if you insert a new row at the boundary. For example, if you add a student's name before ADAMS or after SHAW, the new student's

```
#1         1           2         3         4        5     6      7
 1
 2                    TEST SCORES (PHYSICS)
 3
 4
 5
 6 NAME             TEST1      TEST2     TEST3     TEST4         TOTAL
 7 ===================================================================
 8 ADAMS              54         30        65        51           200
 9 ANSEL              61         31        71        52           215
10 COPPER             49         25        60        43           177
11 DUNN               33         21        49        43           146
12 ETTENGER           52         23        66        47           188
13 JAMIESON           59         28        61        57           205
14 MCMURRY            53         29        57        42           181
15 RADDER             60         29        71        49           209
16 SHAW               44         27        53        40           164
17                 --------   --------  --------  --------      --------
18 AVERAGE SCORE    51.67      27.00     61.44     47.11        140.11
19
20 POSSIBLE SCORE     65         33        80        55           233
```

Figure 7-4. *TEST SCORES worksheet results*

data will not be included in the average score for each test. A better solution here is to have the Name reference ranges for TEST1, TEST2, TEST3, TEST4, and TOTAL include the rows immediately above and below the actual data — in this case, the separator row and the row of dashes following the test scores. The equals signs and dashes in these cells will not affect the calculations, and these range boundaries guarantee that the test data of students added anywhere in the list will automatically be included in the calculations. Given that they help keep calculations correct no matter how you rearrange your worksheet or add or delete data, it is a good idea to allow for these dummy rows and columns on your initial planning sheets. You will be doing this in the remaining worksheets in this book.

You will again work with the TEST SCORES data later in this chapter, but save the worksheet now using the name TESTSCOR.C7. You will want to refer to this version of the worksheet in later chapters.

Using Edit

Sometimes a formula needs only minor changes, as in the last example, where −3 was changed to a −1. The Edit command is convenient for this purpose. To try this command, move the cell pointer over the ADAMS total score, 200, and press Edit. The command line displays

EDIT: SUM(RC[−1]:RC[−5])

The F7, F8, F9, and F10 keys work just as they do when you are entering text with Alpha or formulas with Value. F7 and F8 move the edit cursor left and right a word at a time; F9 and F10 move the cursor left and right a character at a time. Move the cursor over the 1 and use DEL to delete it. Type 3 and press ENTER. The total points displayed in column 7 for ADAMS is 149.

You can also enter the edited formula by pressing an arrow key. The data will be entered in the active cell and the cell pointer moved to the next cell in the direction of the arrow you pressed. You will also remain in Edit mode. Use the Edit command to correct the formula so that the ADAMS score is again 200. A reminder: If you make a mistake in editing a formula and the easier remedy is to start over, you can press ESC to return to the main command menu.

Locking and Unlocking Cells and Formulas

You'll use this worksheet now to become familiar with the Lock command, which lets you "lock" data in certain cells so it cannot be changed or deleted. For example, in the present worksheet you may wish to lock all the cells that contain formulas. You could then blank other portions of the worksheet without the possibility of blanking the formulas by mistake.

Lock/Cells

Move the cell pointer to the home position and press Lock. The command line displays the following:

LOCK: <u>Cells</u> Formulas

The Cells subcommand allows you to lock any individual cell or block of cells on the worksheet. To see how this is done, press ENTER to choose the Cells subcommand, and you are presented with the following display on the command line:

LOCK cells: <u>R1C1</u>   status: Locked (Unlocked)

You're going to lock the section of the worksheet that contains all of the test scores. Move the cell pointer to the first test score, at R8C2. Type a colon and move the cell pointer over the last test score at R16C6. It makes no difference if the Lock command applies to rows or columns that contain blank cells. Press the TAB key to move to the "status:" field and press Locked. Your command line shows the following:

LOCK cells: R8C2:R16C6 _   status: (Locked) Unlocked

Locking cells not only protects data in the locked cell; it also has another effect: It allows you to move the cell pointer quickly to an unlocked cell. To try this, first move the cell pointer to the home position, then press the F2 key to move the cell pointer to the next cell that contains text or data and is not locked. Press the F2 key a few times and watch how the cell pointer moves.

Press F2 until the cell pointer is over the name ADAMS; when you press F2 again, the cell pointer will move across all of the "locked" test data, to the TOTAL column. Pressing F2 again moves the cell pointer over the name ANSEL. If you lock large blocks of text, using F2 can be a quick way to move about among the unlocked cells in your worksheet.

Now consider the other effect of locking cells, protecting data. With the right arrow key, move the cell pointer into the block of cells that you just locked. Move it over the TEST2 score for ANSEL and change this test score to 35. When you press ENTER, notice that the value does not change; instead you hear a beep and the message line displays "Locked cell may not be changed." The Lock command is useful for preventing accidental changes in any section of your worksheet.

You can unlock this block of cells by using the Lock command again. Press **Lock** and ENTER. In the "cells:" field enter (by typing or by using the cell pointer) the same block that you entered previously; press the TAB key to move the edit cursor to the "status:" field and there press **Unlocked**. Press ENTER and your worksheet is back to its original unlocked state. To unlock an entire worksheet with one command, enter the maximum worksheet range R1:255 in the "cells:" field, and in the "status:" field press **Unlocked**.

Lock/Formulas

Let's consider the second Lock subcommand, Formulas. Press **Lock** and **Formulas**. Your command line displays the following:

LOCK FORMULAS:

The message line displays

Enter Y to confirm —

Press **Y** to confirm that you wish to lock all formulas in the worksheet. This command automatically locks all cells that contain a formula or text (Alpha) entry. This means that the cell pointer will move only to cells containing numeric data, such as those in the block containing the actual test scores for an individual test. The cells that display the student totals contain formulas. When looking at a worksheet in this format, it is not obvious which cells contain numeric data and which contain formulas. You do not have the choice of selecting certain formulas. If you decide you don't want to lock formulas, press ENTER to return to the command line.

Like LOCK cells, the LOCK FORMULAS command has two effects. First it prevents you from changing any formulas or text in the worksheet. Second, it has an effect on what cells the cell pointer will move to when F2 is pressed. Pressing F2 causes the cell pointer to move to the next unlocked cell that is not blank.

Try this now. Move the cell pointer to the home position. With LOCK FORMULAS in effect, press F2; the cell pointer should move to the first cell containing numeric data (the number 54, the ADAMS score for TEST1). Experiment using the F2 key to move the cell pointer about the worksheet. This is a fast way to change numeric data entries in a worksheet.

To unlock all the formulas in the worksheet, use the LOCK cells command. Press **L**ock and **C**ells. In the "cells:" field type **R1:255**, press TAB, and in the "status:" field press **U**nlocked. Then press ENTER and the entire worksheet will be unlocked. You can also unlock individual cells by using the LOCK cells command. You would do this if, for example, just one formula in a worksheet needed to be changed.

Displaying Formulas in a Worksheet

You already know that you can view any of your formulas by moving the cell pointer to the cell that contains the formula and inspecting the formula on the status line. You can also view a formula by using the Edit command in a cell. But if viewing formulas cell by cell is not practical, you can view your worksheet on the screen with *all* the formulas displayed. You do this by using the Format/Options command.

Format/Options

Press **F**ormat and **O**ptions. Your command line displays the following:

FORMAT OPTIONS commas: Yes (No)   formulas: Yes (No)

You are interested in the "formulas:" field now, so press the TAB key to move to that field. Press **Y**es. Before you press ENTER, scroll your worksheet so that the screen displays columns 4 through 11 and rows 5 through 24. Press ENTER. Your screen looks like Figure 7-5.

There are a few important points to notice on this display. First, just as when you printed formulas on the printer, the column widths on the screen display have doubled. Complete formulas are displayed in column 7. If you have a worksheet where double column widths are still not wide enough to display the full formula, you can increase the width of the column prior to using the FORMAT OPTIONS command. The maximum column width you can set is 32, which gives a maximum width of 64. The only way to view particularly long formulas may be to use the Edit command.

Another important item to notice is that all text entries are enclosed in quotes, whereas functions, formulas, and names (which may *look* like text entries) are *not* enclosed in quotes. Text entries are shown in rows 6 and 17. In Row 18 the function AVERAGE and the names TEST3 and TEST4 are not displayed in quotes.

```
              "      TEST

"NAME"          "TEST1"   "TEST2"   "TEST3"   "TEST4"      "TOTAL"
"=============="=========="========="========="========="=="=========
"ADAMS"          54        30        65        51          SUM(RC[-2]
"ANSEL"          61        31        71        52          SUM(RC[-2]
"COPPER"         49        25        60        43          SUM(RC[-2]
"DUNN"           33        21        49        43          SUM(RC[-2]
"ETTENGER"       52        23        66        47          SUM(RC[-2]
"JAMIESON"       59        28        61        57          SUM(RC[-2]
"MCMURRY"        53        29        57        42          SUM(RC[-2]
"RADDER"         60        29        71        49          SUM(RC[-2]
"SHAW"           44        27        53        40          SUM(RC[-2]
              "  -------" -------" -------" -------      "  -------
"AVERAGE  SCORE"AVERAGE(TEAVERAGE(TEAVERAGE(TEAVERAGE(TE  AVERAGE(TO

"POSSIBLE  SCORE65        33        80        55          SUM(RC[-2]
```

Figure 7-5. *Worksheet displaying formulas*

The keys used to move the cell pointer or scroll the worksheet work just the same when your worksheet is in this format as when it is in standard format. Experiment with moving the cell pointer and scrolling the worksheet. You may notice that the headings in rows 2, 3, and 4 are incomplete. Only the portion that is in the cell where continuous text was entered is displayed.

To return your worksheet to standard format, again use the FORMAT OPTIONS command and, with the command cursor in the "formulas:" field, press **No** and then ENTER.

Exercises

1. Determine mentally the correct results for each of the following and verify your answers with Multiplan.

    a. $4-7*3$
    b. $3*4/(2+4)$
    c. $2*3^2$
    d. $(11-8)/3+5$

2. Load the TEST SCORES worksheet. This chapter discussed three formulas for determining average scores. You used one of them in the chapter, and now you will use the other two. In row 24 use SUM(TESTX)/9 to determine the average score for each test. In row 26 use SUM(TEXTX)/COUNT(TESTX) to determine the average.

3. Add a new student, MARTIN, with the scores 53, 24, 63, and 48 to the worksheet. The average scores in rows 24 and 26 will not agree. To obtain the correct results, use the Edit command to change 9 to 10 in the formula SUM(TEXTX)/9.

4. Use the COUNT function to determine the number of students in the class. (Remember, COUNT counts numeric data, not text data.)

Working
With Multiple Windows

- Family Budget Worksheet
- Working With Windows
- Changing Windows
- Linking Windows
- Figuring Percents
- Relative Referencing Between Windows

Commands

- WINDOW SPLIT
- Window/Border
- WINDOW CLOSE
- WINDOW TITLES
- GOTO WINDOW

When a worksheet that you are building has become too large to be viewed all at once, entering data can become awkward. The solution is to split the screen into two or more sections so you can view different portions of the worksheet at the same time. Each of these sections of the screen is called a *window*. To master the idea of windows, you will build a worksheet to keep track of a family budget and then enter data into it.

Family Budget Worksheet

Figure 8-1 shows the planning sheet for the family budget worksheet. First let's review the notation used on the worksheet so you can format your screen accordingly.

The numbers in parentheses above the column numbers indicate the width of each column. Rows 1 through 11 are to be formatted continuous. In row 12, the titles enclosed in parentheses, CODE through EARNED, are to be right-justified. Row 13 contains a separator. Parts of columns 5, 6, and 7, which contain the AMOUNTs for checks, INTEREST PAID, and INTEREST EARNED, are to be formatted with two decimal places.

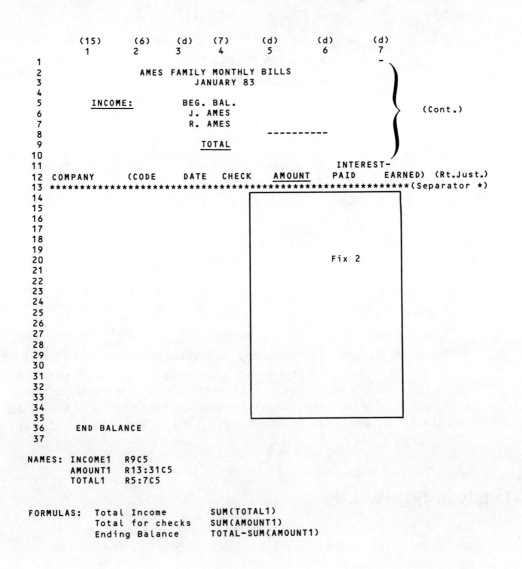

Figure 8-1. *Planning sheet for family budget*

The underlined column headings are to be assigned as Name references. They are also listed at the bottom of the planning sheet, as are the formulas used in the worksheet. The names are created by adding the digit 1 to the column headings. Because the family budget will be calculated monthly, this number distinguishes the entries for each month: 1 for January, 2 for February, and so on. You are going to enter data for a couple of months only, but the method to distinguish all monthly data should be established at the planning stage.

Here's how the family budget worksheet works. Income is calculated as the sum of the month's beginning checkbook balance and the net income of any income earners. Expenses are entered for each payment made within the month. For each expense, the company name or description, date of payment, check number, and amount paid is entered. Interest amounts are tracked separately from the total expense payments so that you can easily total the amount of interest paid or earned each month (this is especially useful for tax purposes). If a check includes interest as part of the payment, enter the full amount paid in the AMOUNT column, and enter the amount of the interest in the INTEREST PAID column. The month's ending balance is the difference between the month's income and expense amounts.

The CODE column is used to categorize each type of expense. The codes you will use are listed in Table 8-1. (In Chapter 11 you will see how to find the sum of only those amounts that have a particular code.)

Format the worksheet now, and enter the titles and formulas. Then enter the sample January data shown in Table 8-2. Use the SUM function in R9C5 to

---

Code   Description

0 = UTILITIES
1 = INTEREST ACCOUNTS
2 = HOME MORTGAGE
3 = STOCK ACCOUNT
4 = MEDICAL
5 = INSURANCE
6 = SAVINGS
7 = FOOD
8 = MISC

Table 8-1. *Expense Codes for Family Budget*

				INTEREST	INTEREST
BEGINNING BALANCE			$ 232.80		
INCOME: J. AMES			1153.87		
R. AMES			1456.77		
COMPANY	DATE	CHECK	AMOUNT	PAID	EARNED
TELEPHONE	01/01	131	23.45		
GAS & ELECTRIC	01/01	132	108.88		
WATER	01/01	133	8.75		
GARBAGE	01/01	134	12.50		
TV CABLE	01/01	135	18.50		
VISA	01/01	136	212.56	17.45	
1st NATIONAL	01/01	137	407.96	396.31	
ALLSTATE (CAR)	01/01	138	243.21		
BLUE CROSS	01/01	139	211.34		
MACY'S	01/01	140	89.03	5.33	
SEARS	01/01	141	156.77	8.93	
SHELL OIL	01/01	142	93.46		
SAFEWAY	01/02	144	95.79		
SAFEWAY	01/09	145	89.71		
CLEANERS	01/09	146	27.34		
SAFEWAY	01/16	147	93.12		
SAFEWAY	01/23	148	99.93		
SAVINGS	01/01	143	450.00		34.98

Table 8-2. *January Data for Family Budget*

determine the total income available for January and in R33C5 to find the total amount spent. Your worksheet should look like Figure 8-2.

Working With Windows

Scroll the worksheet so that columns 4 through 10 and rows 1 through 20 are displayed. Now move your cell pointer to R1C9 and enter the list of expense codes and their descriptions as they appear in Table 8-1. These rows are already

```
         1          2        3       4        5          6          7
 1
 2              AMES FAMILY MONTHLY BILLS
 3                    JANUARY 83
 4
 5       INCOME:      BEG. BAL.          232.8
 6                    J. AMES           1153.87
 7                    R. AMES           1456.77
 8                                     ----------
 9                    TOTAL             2843.44
10
11                                                      INTEREST
12 COMPANY          CODE     DATE   CHECK    AMOUNT     PAID    EARNED
13 ******************************************************************
14 TELEPHONE                01/01    131      23.45
15 GAS & ELECTRIC           01/01    132     108.88
16 WATER                    01/01    133       8.75
17 GARBAGE                  01/01    134      12.50
18 TV CABLE                 01/01    135      18.50
19 VISA                     01/01    136     212.56     17.45
20 1st NATIONAL             01/01    137     407.96    396.31
21 ALLSTATE (CAR)           01/01    138     243.21
22 BLUE CROSS               01/01    139     211.34
23 MACY'S                   01/01    140      89.03      5.33
24 SEARS                    01/01    141     156.77      8.93
25 SHELL OIL                01/01    142      93.46
26 SAFEWAY                  01/02    144      95.79
27 SAFEWAY                  01/09    145      89.71
28 CLEANERS                 01/09    146      27.34
29 SAFEWAY                  01/16    147      93.12
30 SAFEWAY                  01/23    148      99.93
31 SAVINGS                  01/01    143     450.00            34.98
32                                          ----------
33                                           2442.30
34
35
36     END BALANCE
37        $401.14
```

Figure 8-2.   *Initial January family budget worksheet*

formatted continuous, so the code and description will display completely, continuing into column 10.

You can now enter the expense codes in column 2. Move the cell pointer back to column 1. Notice that as you view the company name and code columns, you cannot see the expense codes and descriptions in column 9. It would be helpful, while entering the codes in column 2, to view both column 1, which contains the name of the company to which a check was written, and column 9, which contains the code description. You can do this by defining two *windows* to be displayed on the screen at the same time.

Window/Split

To view two parts of a worksheet, you will split the screen into two windows using the WINDOW SPLIT command. Again scroll so that columns 4 through 10 are displayed. Move the cell pointer to column 9 and press **Window**. Your command line displays the following:

WINDOW: <u>Split</u> Border Close Link Paint

The Split subcommand is highlighted, so press ENTER. The command line now displays

WINDOW SPLIT: <u>Horizontal</u> Vertical Titles

Since you're working with columns, you want Vertical. Press **Vertical**, and your command line displays

WINDOW SPLIT VERTICAL at column: 9   linked: Yes(No)

To create two windows, you want the vertical window split at column 9, which is automatically entered in the "at column:" field because you placed the cell pointer there. You could change the column number, but since it is correct now, press ENTER. (The "linked:" field will be discussed later.) Your screen should now look like Figure 8-3.

```
#1      4         5         6         7        8  #2        9          10
 1                                                 1  CODE
 2 HLY BILLS                                        2  0 = UTILITIES
 3    84                                            3  1 = INTEREST ACCOUNT
 4                                                  4  2 = HOME MORTGAGE
 5              232.8                                5  3 = STOCK ACCOUNT
 6             1153.87                               6  4 = MEDICAL
 7             1456.77                               7  5 = INSURANCE
 8             ----------                            8  6 = SAVINGS
 9             2843.44                               9  7 = FOOD
10                                                 10  8 = MISC
11                            INTEREST             11
12   CHECK    AMOUNT    PAID    EARNED             12
13 ****************************************        13
14   131      23.45                               14
15   132     108.88                               15
16   133       8.75                               16
17   134      12.50                               17
18   135      18.5                                18
19   136     212.56    17.45                      19
20   137     407.96   397.31                      20
```

Figure 8-3.   *Vertically split windows*

The appearance of your screen is changed slightly: the window #2 indicator and a list of row numbers are now displayed at the left edge of the new window, between columns 8 and 9. The window #2 indicator is highlighted, indicating that it is the *active window* (the one containing the cell pointer). Adding a window, as you just did, is sometimes referred to as *opening* a window.

Changing Windows

Let's practice moving the cell pointer in the new window. Press the right arrow key twice, and column 10 in window #2 moves next to column 8 in window #1; column 9 has scrolled *out* of window #2, column 11 has scrolled *into* window #2, and the display in window #1 is unchanged. Move the cell pointer to R21C10,

and you will see row 1 of column 10 scroll off the top of the screen, but row 1 of window #1 remains unchanged. Moving the cell pointer and scrolling window #2 is just the same as when you were working with a single window, except the left arrow key does not allow you to cross from window #2 into window #1.

To move the cell pointer from one window to another, press the F1 key. The cell pointer automatically changes windows. When you press F1, the cell pointer moves to window #1, and the window indicator #1 is highlighted, indicating that window #1 is the active window. Again, window #1 scrolls left, right, up, and down, just as it did previously — except, of course, that its display area is smaller. You can move the cell pointer back to window #2 simply by pressing F1.

With the cell pointer in window #1, use the arrow keys to scroll the contents until the window displays columns 1 through 4 and rows 11 through 30. Move the cell pointer to window #2 and scroll the window so that it displays columns 9 and 10 and rows 1 through 20. With the company names displayed in window #1 and the code descriptions displayed in window #2, it is now convenient to enter the codes. Enter the code for each check as follows. Scroll window #1 up as needed so you can easily compare the codes with their descriptions as you are entering them.

Company	Code	Check
TELEPHONE	0	131
GAS & ELECTRIC	0	132
WATER	0	133
GARBAGE	0	134
TV CABLE	0	135
VISA	1	136
1st NATIONAL	2	137
ALLSTATE (CAR)	5	138
BLUE CROSS	4	139
MACY'S	1	140
SEARS	1	141
SHELL OIL	1	142
SAFEWAY	7	144
SAFEWAY	7	145
CLEANERS	8	146
SAFEWAY	7	147
SAFEWAY	7	148
SAVINGS	6	143

Now scroll window #1 so that it displays rows 15 through 34 and columns 1 through 5; with window #2 still displaying rows 1 through 20 and columns 9 and 10, your screen looks like Figure 8-4.

Window/Border

When more than one window is displayed on the screen, it is sometimes difficult to distinguish quickly between the data in the two (or more) windows.

```
#1          1          2      3      4      5    #2        9          10
   15 GAS & ELECTRIC   0    01/01  132   108.88    1 CODE
   16 WATER            0    01/01  133     8.75    2 0 = UTILITIES
   17 GARBAGE          0    01/01  134    12.50    3 1 = INTEREST ACCOUNT
   18 TV CABLE         0    01/01  135    18.5     4 2 = HOME MORTGAGE
   19 VISA             1    01/01  136   212.56    5 3 = STOCK ACCOUNT
   20 1st NATIONAL     2    01/01  137   407.96    6 4 = MEDICAL
   21 ALLSTATE (CAR)   5    01/01  138   243.21    7 5 = INSURANCE
   22 BLUE CROSS       4    01/01  139   211.34    8 6 = SAVINGS
   23 MACY'S           1    01/01  140    89.03    9 7 = FOOD
   24 SEARS            1    01/01  141   156.77   10 8 = MISC
   25 SHELL OIL        1    01/01  142    93.46   11
   26 SAFEWAY          7    01/02  144    95.79   12
   27 SAFEWAY          7    01/09  145    89.71   13
   28 CLEANERS         8    01/09  146    27.34   14
   29 SAFEWAY          7    01/16  147    93.12   15
   30 SAFEWAY          7    01/23  148    99.93   16
   31 SAVINGS          6    01/01  143   450.00   17
   32                                ----------   18
   33                                    2442.30  19
   34                                             20
```

Figure 8-4. *Split windows scrolled to different rows*

Multiplan provides a solution for this: you can enclose your windows (either individually or all of them) with borders. Let's try this. Keep your screen display the same as in Figure 8-4, and with the cell pointer in window #1, press **Window** and **B**order from the submenu. The command line displays the following:

WINDOW change border in window number: <u>1</u>

The number 1 is highlighted in the "window number:" field, because the cell pointer is in that window. Press ENTER and window #1 is enclosed by a border. Move the cell pointer to window #2 and follow the same procedure to form a border around window #2. Your screen now looks like Figure 8-5.

Notice that when a window is enclosed by a border, two rows fewer are displayed. Also, if the full width of a column cannot be displayed at the edge of a window, the entire column will be lost from the display, as happened here to column 5 in window #1.

To *release*, or erase, the window borders, you again use the Window/Border command. Press **Window** and **B**order, and in the "window number:" field enter the number of the window from which you wish the border removed. This command is a *toggle:* if the border is on, the command turns it off; if the border is off, the command turns it on. Return the borders to both windows.

```
#1          1         2      3      4        #2        9          10
15 GAS & ELECTRIC     0    01/01  132        1 CODE
16 WATER              0    01/01  133        2 0 = UTILITIES
17 GARBAGE            0    01/01  134        3 1 = INTEREST ACCOUNT
18 TV CABLE           0    01/01  135        4 2 = HOME MORTGAGE
19 VISA               1    01/01  136        5 3 = STOCK ACCOUNT
20 1st NATIONAL       2    01/01  137        6 4 = MEDICAL
21 ALLSTATE (CAR)     5    01/01  138        7 5 = INSURANCE
22 BLUE CROSS         4    01/01  139        8 6 = SAVINGS
23 MACY'S             1    01/01  140        9 7 = FOOD
24 SEARS              1    01/01  141       10 8 = MISC
25 SHELL OIL          1    01/01  142       11
26 SAFEWAY            7    01/02  144       12
27 SAFEWAY            7    01/09  145       13
28 CLEANERS           8    01/09  146       14
29 SAFEWAY            7    01/16  147       15
30 SAFEWAY            7    01/23  148       16
31 SAVINGS            6    01/01  143       17
32                                          18
```

Figure 8-5. *Windows with borders*

With window #1 displaying columns 1 through 4 and rows 11 through 28, move the cell pointer to row 14. When worksheets become lengthy, it is often convenient to create a window to display column titles on the screen. That is, you make a narrow horizontal window at the top of the screen that incorporates the column headings. Normally, you will want this window to be a minimum of three rows so that if you wish to put a border around it, at least one row will be left for the display. Press **Window, Split,** and **Horizontal.** The "at row:" field contains the correct value, 14, so press ENTER. The screen looks like Figure 8-6.

Notice that the windows have been renumbered. Window #1 becomes #3, and the new window becomes #1. Column numbers are added to window #3. The new window initially appears with a border because it was split from the old window #1, which was displayed with a border earlier. If a window enclosed by a border is split, the border is transferred to both windows.

Again use the F1 key to move the cell pointer from one window to the next. Notice that it moves from window to window in numerical order, in a clockwise circular fashion. It's possible to scroll within any window through the entire worksheet.

```
#1          1          2       3       4          #2      9          10
11                                                 1 CODE
12 COMPANY             CODE    DATE    CHECK        2 0 = UTILITIES
13 ************************************             3 1 = INTEREST ACCOUNT
                                                   4 2 = HOME MORTGAGE
                                                   5 3 = STOCK ACCOUNT
#3          1          2       3       4           6 4 = MEDICAL
14 TELEPHONE           0       01/01   131         7 5 = INSURANCE
15 GAS & ELECTRIC      0       01/01   132         8 6 = SAVINGS
16 WATER               0       01/01   133         9 7 = FOOD
17 GARBAGE             0       01/01   134        10 8 = MISC
18 TV CABLE            0       01/01   135        11
19 VISA                1       01/01   136        12
20 1st NATIONAL        2       01/01   137        13
21 ALLSTATE (CAR)      5       01/01   138        14
22 BLUE CROSS          4       01/01   139        15
23 MACY'S              1       01/01   140        16
24 SEARS               1       01/01   141        17
25 SHELL OIL           1       01/01   142        18
```

Figure 8-6.   *Third window added (#1) to show column heads*

Window/Close

To remove, or *close*, a window, you use the WINDOW CLOSE command. Move the cell pointer to window #1 and press **W**indow and **C**lose. Your command line reads

WINDOW CLOSE window number:1

Press ENTER and window #1 is eliminated. Notice that the remaining two windows are renumbered 1 and 2. Regardless of which window is closed, the remaining windows will always be renumbered to begin with 1 and will continue in sequence to the highest number of windows you have. Multiplan allows up to eight windows to be opened on a worksheet.

Now close window #2. Whether you close window #1 or #2, you still end up with a single window numbered #1. The only difference is data displayed on the screen; it will be that from the window left open. Erase the border now, and your screen returns to its original format, a single window without a border.

A couple of additional notes about windows: First, if you save your worksheet with multiple windows open, the same windows will be open when you reload the worksheet at a later time. Second, any of the windows (whether one, some, or all of them) that have borders when the worksheet is saved will have them when the worksheet is reloaded.

Linking Windows

Up to this point, when you have created windows, the "linked:" field was left in its default setting, No. At times it is convenient to link windows so that they scroll together, either vertically or horizontally. Try this now. Scroll the worksheet so that columns 1 through 7 and rows 9 through 28 are displayed, and follow these steps:

1. Place the cell pointer over TELEPHONE, in R14C1.
2. Press **Window** and ENTER for Split.
3. Horizontal is correct, so press ENTER.
4. You want the window to split at row 14, so the entry there is correct. Press TAB to move to the "linked:" field. Press the space bar or **Yes** to highlight Yes and then press ENTER.
5. Move the cell pointer into window #1 and enclose it with a border.
6. Scroll window #1 so that rows 11, 12, and 13 are displayed.

When you were scrolling window #1 vertically, there was no change in window #2. Notice also that there is only one set of column numbers for the two windows. This is all that is necessary since both windows will scroll together horizontally. To see this effect, move the cell pointer to window #2, and using either the SCROLL LOCK (described in Chapter 1) or the right arrow key, scroll the screen. There is a short delay before window #1 also scrolls so that the columns for both windows #1 and #2 remain aligned. Close window #1; you're going to try linking windows so that they scroll together vertically.

Scroll the worksheet to display columns 1 through 7 and rows 11 through 30. Move the cell pointer into column 2 and select the WINDOW SPLIT command. With the WINDOW SPLIT command line displayed, press Vertical. The 2 in the "at column:" field is correct, so press the TAB key to move to the "linked:" field and then press **Yes** so the windows will be linked. Now press ENTER. You again have two windows. Notice there are two sets of column numbers but only one set of row numbers. To see the column numbers clearly, move the cell pointer to column 8 and press the right arrow key. You can see that window #2 scrolls left while window #1 remains stationary. Press the HOME key so the cell pointer is in R11C3 of window #2. Now press the up arrow key. You can see that as window #2 scrolls down, window #1 also scrolls down. Press the PGUP and PGDN keys and you'll notice that the windows are linked for movement of a full screen of data, as well as for individual rows.

Now remove all windows and borders.

Window/Titles

In addition to creating windows and then choosing whether or not to link them, you can simultaneously create and link windows by using the WINDOW SPLIT TITLES command. This command allows you to split the screen into either two or four windows that are automatically linked.

Let's first split the screen into two linked windows. To try this, scroll your worksheet so that columns 1 through 7 and rows 11 through 30 are on the screen. Move the cell pointer over TELEPHONE and press **W**indow, **S**plit, and **T**itle. The command line displays

WINDOW SPLIT TITLES: # of rows: 3   # of columns: 0

The default value 3 appears in the "# of rows:" field because there are three rows above the cell pointer. The value 0 appears in the "# of columns:" field because there are zero columns to the left of the cell pointer. These are the values you wish, so press ENTER. The screen is divided into two windows as shown in Figure 8-7. You can tell the windows are linked to scroll together horizontally because there is only one set of column numbers. With the SCROLL LOCK key or the arrow keys, scroll the screen to confirm that they are linked.

Now let's try using this command to split the screen vertically. Close the previous window and move the cell pointer to R11C2. Again press **W**indow, **S**plit, and **T**itles. The default values in the fields on the command line are correct because of where you placed your cell pointer, so press ENTER. You now have a vertical split, with a single set of row numbers and a split set of column numbers; therefore, your windows will scroll together vertically but not horizontally. Scroll the screen to confirm this.

Now let's divide the screen into four windows. Again, close the previous window, and with columns 1 through 7 and rows 11 through 30 displayed on the

```
#1           1         2      3      4        5           6         7
  11                                                             INTEREST
  12 COMPANY            CODE   DATE   CHECK    AMOUNT      PAID    EARNED
  13 ************************************************************************
#2
  14 TELEPHONE          0      01/01  131      23.45
  15 GAS & ELECTRIC     0      01/01  132      108.88
  16 WATER              0      01/01  133      8.75
  17 GARBAGE            0      01/01  134      12.50
  18 TV CABLE           0      01/01  135      18.5
  19 VISA               1      01/01  136      212.56      17.45
  20 1st NATIONAL       2      01/01  137      407.96      397.31
  21 ALLSTATE (CAR)     5      01/01  138      243.21
  22 BLUE CROSS         4      01/01  139      211.34
  23 MACY'S             1      01/01  140      89.03                 5.33
  24 SEARS              1      01/01  141      156.77               8.93
  25 SHELL OIL          1      01/01  142      93.46
  26 SAFEWAY            7      01/02  144      95.79
  27 SAFEWAY            7      01/09  145      89.71
  28 CLEANERS           8      01/09  146      27.34
  29 SAFEWAY            7      01/16  147      93.12
```

Figure 8-7. *Screen divided by WINDOW SPLIT TITLES command*

screen, move the cell pointer to R14C2. Press **Window, Split,** and **Titles,** and your command line displays

WINDOW SPLIT TITLES: # of rows: 3   # of columns: 1

Press ENTER; the screen splits both vertically and horizontally from the current location of the cell pointer, and all windows are linked. The screen now looks like Figure 8-8.

This command links the windows automatically. Windows #2 and #3 have a common set of column numbers, so they will scroll together horizontally. Windows #1 and #4 are also linked and will scroll together horizontally. Windows #3 and #4 have a common set of row numbers, so they will scroll together vertically. Windows #1 and #2 will also scroll together vertically.

In Figure 8-9 the arrows on the common borders indicate how the windows are linked to scroll together. The window pairs 1 and 2 and 3 and 4 scroll together vertically, while the pairs 1 and 4 and 2 and 3 scroll together horizontally.

When your screen is divided into four windows, it is usually worthwhile to place borders on them. With the screen already split as it is now, you would have

```
#1              1        #2    2       3      4       5       6           7
11                                                                   INTEREST
12  COMPANY                     CODE    DATE   CHECK   AMOUNT      PAID    EARNED
13  ***************             ********************************************************
#4                       #3
14  TELEPHONE                   0       01/01  131      23.45
15  GAS & ELECTRIC              0       01/01  132     108.88
16  WATER                       0       01/01  133       8.75
17  GARBAGE                     0       01/01  134      12.50
18  TV CABLE                    0       01/01  135      18.5
19  VISA                        1       01/01  136     212.56      17.45
20  1st NATIONAL                2       01/01  137     407.96     397.31
21  ALLSTATE (CAR)              5       01/01  138     243.21
22  BLUE CROSS                  4       01/01  139     211.34
23  MACY'S                      1       01/01  140      89.03       5.33
24  SEARS                       1       01/01  141     156.77       8.93
25  SHELL OIL                   1       01/01  142      93.46
26  SAFEWAY                     7       01/02  144      95.79
27  SAFEWAY                     7       01/09  145      89.71
28  CLEANERS                    8       01/09  146      27.34
29  SAFEWAY                     7       01/16  147      93.12
```

Figure 8-8.   *Screen divided into four windows by WINDOW SPLIT TITLES command*

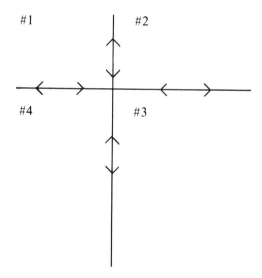

Figure 8-9.   *Scrolling patterns of linked windows*

to use the Window/Border command four times in order to place a border on each of the windows. If you know in advance that you want borders, the easiest thing to do is to enter a border on window #1 before entering the WINDOW SPLIT command. Then when you split the screen into four windows, each window will have a border.

When four windows are created by use of the Titles command, then regardless of which window the cell pointer is in, using the WINDOW CLOSE command will leave only one window open. The cell pointer can be in any window when you do this. To return the screen to a single window, press **W**indow and **C**lose. To remove the border, press **W**indow, **B**order, and ENTER.

Goto/Window

When working with large worksheets and multiple windows, you may find the GOTO WINDOW command useful. By entering only one command you can move to any cell in any window. Let's try this command now.

With rows 1 through 20 and columns 1 through 7 displayed, move the cell pointer to column 6 and split the screen vertically. With the cell pointer in R6C6 of window #2, press **G**oto and **W**indow. The command line displays

GOTO WINDOW window number:2   row:6   column:6

The default field values identify the current position of the cell pointer. To move to R12C1 of window #1, change the field values to match the following command line:

GOTO WINDOW window number:1   row:12   column:1

Press ENTER. The cell pointer immediately moves to window #1, which is scrolled so that R12C1 becomes the home position. You may use this command to move from any window to any particular cell in another window or to any particular cell in the same window. When you move the pointer to another window, that window becomes the active window.

The distinction between the GOTO WINDOW command and the GOTO/Row-col command is important and useful: With the GOTO WINDOW command, the cell pointer goes to the designated cell and that cell moves to become the home position of the window. By contrast, with the GOTO/Row-col command, the cell pointer goes to the designated cell, but the position of data on the screen does not move. Note that you can use the GOTO WINDOW command even when only a single window is on the screen in order to scroll the worksheet automatically so the designated cell is in the home position.

Again clear all the windows and borders from this worksheet; then save it under the filename BUDGET.C8. You will use it again in Chapter 10.

Figuring Percents

Load in the TEST SCORES worksheet from the last chapter. Let's add to this worksheet a column that determines the percent of questions correct for each student.

In preparation, split the screen vertically into two windows at column 2. Scroll the contents of window #2 so that your screen looks like Figure 8-10.

Move the cell pointer to R6C8 and enter the heading PERCENT. Use the Name command and assign the name PERCENT to rows 7 through 17 of column 8. Continue the separator (=) under PERCENT.

With the FORMAT cells command, change rows 8 through 16 of column 8 to the percent format. When a cell or block is formatted to find percent, Multiplan automatically multiplies the value computed for each cell by 100, to change the

```
#1            1        #2   6      7        8         9         10        11
 5
 6 NAME                          TOTAL
 7 ================      ================
 8 ADAMS                           200
 9 ANSEL                           215
10 COPPER                          177
11 DUNN                            146
12 ETTENGER                        188
13 JAMIESON                        205
14 MCMURRY                         181
15 RADDER                          209
16 SHAW                            164
17                              --------
18 AVERAGE SCORE                187.22
19
20 POSSIBLE SCORE                  233
21
22
23
24
```

Figure 8-10. *Window #2 scrolled horizontally to receive new column*

decimal fraction to a percent. The command line should look like this:

FORMAT cells: R8C8:R16C8   alignment:(Def)Ctr Gen Left Right —
format code: Def Cont Èxp Fix Gen Int $ * (%) — # of decimals: 2

Now move the cell pointer to R20C7, over the total number of points possible (233). Use the Name command to name this cell. Since there is no text in the cell, when you press **Name**, the "define name:" field is blank. Enter the Name reference, TOTALPTS, standing for total points. The reference R20C7 is correct, so press ENTER.

Each student's percentage is determined by dividing that student's total number of points by the total possible for all the tests and then multiplying by 100. ADAMS earned a total of 200 points. Since the total possible on all tests is 233, the result of $200/233 \times 100$ gives the percent for ADAMS. In Multiplan notation the formula is

$$RC[-1]/TOTALPTS$$

represents 233

represents 200

You do not have to multiply by 100 since column 7 is formatted to calculate percent; this automatically multiplies the result of 200/233 by 100. Enter the formula, press ENTER, and then copy the formula to the eight rows below. Move the cell pointer to R17C8 and enter the line of dashes. Move the cell pointer down one row and enter the formula to figure the average percent. Using functions, this formula is

AVERAGE(PERCENT)

Press ENTER and the screen looks like Figure 8-11.

Using a two-window display makes it easy to see the percentage each student achieved on the tests.

Relative Referencing Between Windows

Sometimes when you enter a formula the cells that contain the data for that formula may be in some distant part of the worksheet. It then becomes inconvenient to move the cell pointer to the desired data cell, and there is a greater

#1	1	#2	7	8	9	10	11
5		5					
6	NAME	6	TOTAL	PERCENT			
7	===============	7	=============================				
8	ADAMS	8	200	85.84%			
9	ANSEL	9	215	92.27%			
10	COPPER	10	177	75.97%			
11	DUNN	11	146	62.66%			
12	ETTENGER	12	188	80.69%			
13	JAMIESON	13	205	87.98%			
14	MCMURRY	14	181	77.68%			
15	RADDER	15	209	89.70%			
16	SHAW	16	164	70.39%			
17		17	--------	--------			
18	AVERAGE SCORE	18	187.22	80.35%			
19		19					
20	POSSIBLE SCORE	20	233				
21		21					
22		22					
23		23					
24		24					

Figure 8-11. *Two-window screen with new column to receive percents*

chance for error. You can solve this problem by using windows. To see how, you'll have to enter the formulas for determining the test score percents in another section of the worksheet.

As an example, first use the **C**opy command to copy the names in column 1 down the worksheet to a position starting in row 25. Press the PGDN key so that the screen displays rows 21 through 40. Enter the separator so that it is in columns 1 and 2 by formatting row 26 continuous for those columns. Enter the title PERCENT in column 2. Your screen should look the same as Figure 8-12.

Just as you did in "Figuring Percents," format column 2, rows 27 through 35, to calculate percents.

Press the PGUP key and scroll the screen so rows 1 through 20 and columns 4 through 11 are displayed. Move the cell pointer into column 8 and use the Window command to split the screen vertically. With the cell pointer in window #2, use the GOTO/Row-col command to go to R26C1 and scroll window #2 so that it matches Figure 8-13.

Now place the cell pointer in R27C2 under PERCENT and use the Value command to enter the same formula for percent that you used previously. While in the Value command, press F1 to move into window #1. Place the cell pointer over 200 in the TOTAL column. Even though you apparently moved only two

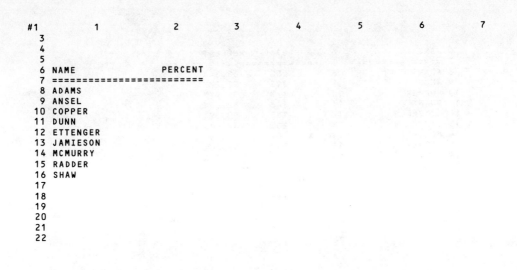

```
#1           1           2           3           4           5           6           7
    3
    4
    5
    6 NAME                PERCENT
    7 ============================
    8 ADAMS
    9 ANSEL
   10 COPPER
   11 DUNN
   12 ETTENGER
   13 JAMIESON
   14 MCMURRY
   15 RADDER
   16 SHAW
   17
   18
   19
   20
   21
   22
```

Figure 8-12.   *Worksheet prepared to receive percents by relative referencing*

```
#1           4           5           6           7  #2           1           2           3
    1                                                  20 POSSIBLE SCORE          65          33
    2 ES                                               21
    3 D                                                22
    4 R 83                                             23
    5                                                  24
    6        TEST3       TEST4       TOTAL  25 NAME                PERCENT
    7 ==================================== 26 ============================
    8          65          51         200  27 ADAMS
    9          71          52         215  28 ANSEL
   10          60          43         177  29 COPPER
   11          49          43         146  30 DUNN
   12          66          47         188  31 ETTENGER
   13          61          57         205  32 JAMIESON
   14          57          42         181  33 MCMURRY
   15          71          49         209  34 RADDER
   16          53          40         164  35 SHAW
   17    --------    --------    -------- 36
   18       61.44       47.11      187.22 37
   19                                      38
   20          80          55         233  39
```

Figure 8-13.   *Vertically split windows with #2 scrolled to receive percents*

```
#1        5       6       7        8   #2           1              2        3
 1                                     20  POSSIBLE  SCORE              65       33
 2                                     21
 3                                     22
 4                                     23
 5                                     24
 6        TEST4           TOTAL   PERCENT 25  NAME                 PERCENT
 7   ===============================  26  ============================
 8         51             200     85.84% 27  ADAMS                 85.84%
 9         52             215     92.27% 28  ANSEL                 92.27%
10         43             177     75.97% 29  COPPER                75.97%
11         43             146     62.66% 30  DUNN                  62.66%
12         47             188     80.69% 31  ETTENGER              80.69%
13         57             205     87.98% 32  JAMIESON              87.98%
14         42             181     77.68% 33  MCMURRY               77.68%
15         49             209     89.70% 34  RADDER                89.70%
16         40             164     70.39% 35  SHAW                  70.39%
17   --------        --------   -------- 36
18        47.11           187.22  80.35% 37
19                                       38
20         55             233             39
```

Figure 8-14. *Calculations executed by relative referencing between windows*

columns to the left, notice the relative reference on the command line: R[−19]C[+5]. This is the relative position of 200 from the actual position of these names on the worksheet. Enter the division symbol, and the cell pointer immediately moves back to the PERCENT column of window #2. Press the F3 key and the right arrow key until the appropriate name, TOTALPTS, is displayed, and press ENTER. Complete the column just as you did before by copying the formula down eight cells. Your screen now looks like Figure 8-14.

You will find it very useful in many of your worksheets to build formulas by using relative referencing and moving the cell pointer short distances from one window to another.

Save this worksheet—you will use it again.

Exercises

1. Load the family budget worksheet. Split the screen into two vertical windows. Scroll the portion displayed in window #1 to the CODE table and that in window #2 to display the company name and code.

2. Practice placing and removing borders on the windows of Exercise 1.

3. Load the TEST SCORES worksheet, place the cell pointer in R8C2, and with the WINDOW SPLIT TITLES command, split the screen into four windows. Practice scrolling the windows to be sure you understand how they are linked.

4. With the four windows from Exercise 3, practice using the GOTO WINDOW command. After you have tried this a few times, predict the display in affected windows and use the command to verify your predictions.

5. Find the sum of the utility bills (code 0) that the Ames family paid in January. Divide the screen into two windows and build your formula by using the technique of relative referencing between windows. Make the results appear in R1C15.

Graphing Data
And Generating Reports

- Graphing Data
- Using the REPT Function
- Printing Titled Reports
- Sorting Data
- Using REPT to Enter a Separator
- Saving a Worksheet as a Word-Processing File

Commands

- SORT
- PRINT/FILE

Functions

- REPT

In Chapter 5 you were introduced to the commands for printing all or part of a worksheet. In this chapter you'll learn in more detail how to manipulate your data to generate useful reports and how to represent data graphically. You'll start by learning how to use Multiplan's graphing capabilities.

Graphing Data

Let's start by graphing a set of numbers. Clear your screen and use the FORMAT WIDTH command to change the width of column 1 to 4 characters. Now you'll format column 2 so it will graph the data instead of printing numbers. Select the FORMAT cells command. In the "cells:" field type **C2**. Press TAB, and when the edit cursor reaches the "alignment:" field, enter **L** to left-justify the data. Press TAB again to move to the "format code:" field, and enter an asterisk. The asterisk in the "format code:" field is what selects the graphing capability. The command line displays

FORMAT: cells: C2   alignment: Def Ctr(Left)Right —
    format code: Def Cont Exp Fix Gen Int $(*)%—   # of decimals:

Now type the following values in column 1, rows 1 through 10: **4**, **9**, **10**, **7**, **5**, **8**, **11**, **15**, **6**, **18**. Move the cell pointer to R1C2, press **Value**, and move the cell pointer to R1C1. The command line displays

Value: RC[−1]

When you press ENTER, four asterisks, left-justified, are displayed in column 2. This is the graphic representation of the value 4 in R1C1. Copy this formula down nine rows, and your screen should display graphs for the remaining numbers in the column:

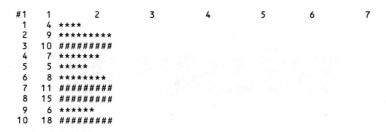

```
#1    1          2          3          4          5          6          7
 1    4  ****
 2    9  *********
 3   10  ########
 4    7  *******
 5    5  *****
 6    8  ********
 7   11  ########
 8   15  ########
 9    6  ******
10   18  ########
```

The numbers 9 or less are represented by asterisks in column 2. If a value in column 1 is larger than 9, number signs (#) are printed in column 2 to indicate there is insufficient room to graph the data. Multiplan does this because the current column width is 10 characters. Notice in row 3 that even though column 2 is 10 characters wide, Multiplan still requires that empty space on the right of the column. Therefore the number signs are printed instead of asterisks for the number 10.

You can change the width of column 2 in order to graph the data accurately. Using the FORMAT WIDTH command, change the width of column 2 to the maximum, 32. All of your data should now be graphed completely.

```
#1    1                    2                    3          4
 1    4  ****
 2    9  *********
 3   10  **********
 4    7  *******
 5    5  *****
 6    8  ********
 7   11  ***********
 8   15  ***************
 9    6  ******
10   18  ******************
```

Scaling Your Graphs

Even with a column width of 32 characters, the numbers you want to graph may be too large to fit the column. One way to correct this is to reduce all the numbers in the same proportion. For example, change the numbers in column 1 to the following: **27, 43, 37, 25, 41, 38, 31, 36, 35, 29.** Even at maximum column width, several of the rows in column 2 are filled with number signs. To correct this, reduce the values in column 1 by half: move the cursor to R1C2, press Edit, and divide the reference to RC[−1] by 2. Your command line now reads

EDIT: RC[−1]/2

Press ENTER and copy the formula down the remaining nine rows. Your screen now should look like this:

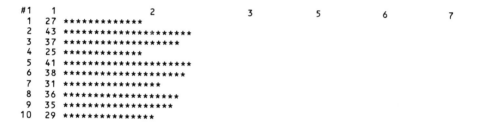

All of the numbers are now graphed accurately. Although the number of asterisks does not equal the value, each value is graphed in correct *proportion* to the others. This process of changing data by a proportion is called scaling. *Scaling down,* as in the example, is dividing data by a value so it will display in an area of limited size: the graph represents one-half the actual data. Scaling is very useful in graphing values that are too large to fit in the column or are so large that the resulting strings of asterisks are uninformative.

Of course you can also *scale up*, or increase the length of the strings of asterisks. To increase the length, you multiply the data by a constant instead of dividing. Scaling up is often useful when the values to be graphed are very small.

Graphing Decimals

When Multiplan encounters decimals among data to be graphed, it rounds them to the nearest whole number. For example, all of the following numbers would be rounded to a value of 1:

$$1.1 \quad 0.9$$
$$1.3 \quad 1.4$$
$$0.8 \quad 0.6$$

If these numbers were in a graph, they each would be represented by one asterisk—and the graph would not be very useful. But if they were first multiplied by 10, the values would stay in proportion and range from 6 to 14 asterisks, creating a far more accurate graph.

Using the REPT Function

You can also graph data by using the REPT (for "repeat") function. REPT has the format REPT("T", Count), where T stands for the text to be repeated and Count is the number of times to repeat the text. The text may be a phrase, but more commonly it is a symbol. Whatever it is, it must be enclosed in double quotation marks.

You'll graph the same set of data as before, this time using the REPT function and the plus sign (+). Before you use this function, change the width of column 2 back to 10.

Place the cell pointer in R1C2, and with the Value command, enter the following formula:

VALUE: REPT("+",RC[−1])

Press ENTER and again copy the formula down the remaining nine rows.

Use the FORMAT cells command and format rows 1 through 10, columns 2 through 5, to be continuous. When the rows are formatted continuous, each value should be fully graphed. The screen display should appear as follows:

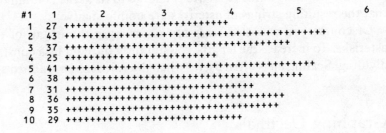

The REPT function has two advantages over the previous graphing method: first, you can choose any character for the symbol in your graph, and second, you can display a string of as many as 255 characters in a row. Note that you could not have used the Cont command with the previous graphs because they were formatted with the Format command: both Cont and * are in the "format code:" field, and only one choice can be made in a single field.

In the next few sections you'll combine these concepts with other Multiplan features to produce specialized reports.

Printing Titled Reports

Load in the TEST SCORES worksheet PHY.MP. Using the Delete command, delete column 8. Your screen should now look like Figure 9-1.

Let's start by printing a portion of the worksheet and giving it a title. Suppose you want to print the names of the students in a list titled 2d PERIOD PHYSICS. To begin, move the cell pointer to R6C1, over NAME, and from the command menu press **P**rinter and **O**ptions. Enter the data shown in the "area:" and "setup:" fields as follows:

PRINT OPTIONS: area: R6C1:R16C1   setup: 2d PERIOD
                                                 PHYSICS
          formulas: Yes(No)   row-col numbers: Yes(No)

```
?
#1       1          2        3        4        5    6    7
 1
 2                     TEST SCORES (PHYSICS)
 3                     SECOND PERIOD
 4                     FIRST SEMESTER 83
 5
 6 NAME              TEST1     TEST2    TEST3    TEST4        TOTAL
 7 ==============================================================
 8 ADAMS               54        30       65       51          200
 9 ANSEL               61        31       71       52          215
10 COPPER              49        25       60       43          177
11 DUNN                33        21       49       43          146
12 ETTENGER            52        23       66       47          188
13 JAMIESON            59        28       61       57          205
14 MCMURRY             53        29       57       42          181
15 RADDER              60        29       71       49          209
16 SHAW                44        27       53       40          164
17                  --------  -------- -------- --------     --------
18 AVERAGE SCORE     51.67     27.00    61.44    47.11       187.22
19
20 POSSIBLE SCORE      65        33       80       55          233
```

Figure 9-1. *TEST SCORES worksheet*

The "formulas:" and "row-col numbers:" fields are correct, so press ENTER. With the Printer subcommand highlighted, again press ENTER (make sure your printer is turned on and ready to print). The printed report is shown in Figure 9-2.

The space between the title 2d PERIOD PHYSICS and the title NAME can be changed with the PRINT MARGINS subcommand by entering a smaller number in the "top:" field. The title you enter in the "setup:" field can be a maximum of 19 characters.

When entering data in the "setup:" field, you will find it useful to (1) add the date, particularly when a worksheet is printed frequently, so you can quickly identify the latest copy; (2) print the filename to remind yourself where the worksheet can be found on your disk. This last step is especially useful when you work with a large number of files.

Sorting Data

A common way of organizing a list, like that of students' names, is by alphabetical order. Often, though, it may be more useful to rank data from highest to lowest. This is easy to do with Multiplan's Sort command, one of its most powerful report-generating tools.

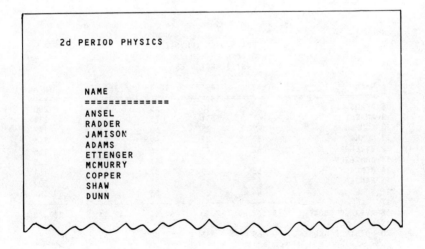

Figure 9-2. *Printed worksheet with title*

```
              1              2          3          4        5    6    7
         1
         2                       TEST SCORES (PHYSICS)
         3                          SECOND PERIOD
         4                        FIRST SEMESTER 83
         5
         6  NAME               TEST1      TEST2      TEST3    TEST4      TOTAL
         7  ===========================================================
         8  ANSEL                61         31         71       52         215
         9  RADDER               60         29         71       49         209
        10  JAMIESON             59         28         61       57         205
        11  ADAMS                54         30         65       51         200
        12  ETTENGER             52         23         66       47         188
        13  MCMURRY              53         29         57       42         181
        14  COPPER               49         25         60       43         177
        15  SHAW                 44         27         53       40         164
        16  DUNN                 33         21         49       43         146
        17                     --------   --------   --------  --------   --------
        18  AVERAGE SCORE      51.67      27.00      61.44    47.11      187.22
        19
        20  POSSIBLE SCORE       65         33         80       55         233
```

Figure 9-3. *Test scores sorted in descending order*

Multiplan allows you to sort rows of data in any specified section of the worksheet. In the first example you'll rank the students according to their total test scores.

Move your cell pointer to R8C7 over 200. Press **S**ort and the command line displays the following:

SORT by column: 7   between rows: and: order:($>$)$<$

You are going to sort the section of the worksheet that contains the students' names and data, rows 8 through 16 and columns 1 through 7. The 7 in the "by column:" field is correct, so press the TAB key to move to the "between rows:" field. Type **8**, move to the "and:" field, and type **16**. Move the command cursor now to the last field, "order:", and notice the two symbols $>$ and $<$. You can sort the data from smallest to largest (ascending order) by selecting the greater-than symbol ($>$). Or you can sort the data from largest to smallest (descending order) by selecting the less-than symbol ($<$). Say you prefer descending order; press $<$ and then ENTER. The entire student list is rearranged according to the values in column 7. Your screen now looks like Figure 9-3.

Note that if you wish to print the entire screen, you will have to go back to the PRINT OPTIONS subcommand and change the data in the "area:" field.

The Sort command can be used to sort alphabetic as well as numeric data. To put the students' names back in alphabetical order, move the cell pointer to R8C1, over ANSEL, and press Sort. All the values in the Sort command line are retained from your last entry, except that the last field automatically changes to ascending order. The field entries are correct, so press ENTER. The test scores data is again arranged according to the alphabetic order of student names.

Now let's graph the students' scores. Scroll your TEST SCORES worksheet so that columns 1 through 7 and rows 5 through 24 are displayed. Move the cell pointer to column 2 and split the screen vertically into two windows. Press Window and Split; then move the command cursor to the "linked:" field and press Yes so the windows are linked. Press ENTER.

Scroll window #2 so that it displays columns 7 through 11. Your screen should look like Figure 9-4.

You will graph the TOTAL scores. To give yourself the maximum space to display this graph, use the FORMAT WIDTH command to format column 8 to its maximum width, 32. Use the FORMAT cells command to format the block R8C8:R16C8 to print asterisks. Now move the cell pointer to R8C8. Even though you've set the width of column 8 to the maximum, it's still not wide enough to graph the values from column 7. You'll have to scale down the values.

The largest value in column 7 is 215. What you need is the largest value that when divided into 215 will yield a result at least one less than the column width,

```
#1              1        #2      7          8         9         10        11
   5
   6  NAME                      TOTAL
   7  ================        ================
   8  ADAMS                      200
   9  ANSEL                      215
  10  COPPER                     177
  11  DUNN                       146
  12  ETTENGER                   188
  13  JAMIESON                   205
  14  MCMURRY                    181
  15  RADDER                     209
  16  SHAW                       164
  17                           --------
  18  AVERAGE SCORE             187.22
  19
  20  POSSIBLE SCORE             233
  21
  22
  23
  24
```

Figure 9-4. *Vertically split windows scrolled and linked*

32. The largest divisor you can use and still come up with a value less than 32 is 7. So with the cell pointer in R8C8, press the = key and the right arrow key to move the cell pointer to R8C7. Press the / key and type a 7. Your command line displays the following:

VALUE: RC[−1]/7

Press ENTER and column 8 displays a row of asterisks. Copy the formula down to the eight rows below. Your graph is now complete and should look like Figure 9-5.

You can always print the data on the screen by pressing the SHIFT and PRTSC keys; but if you use the Print/Printer commands from Multiplan, you can print not only what is on the screen, but all the test data in columns 2, 3, 4, and 5.

Close window #2 so that you again have a single window display.

Using REPT to Enter a Separator

Another way to use the REPT function is to enter a separator, as in row 7 of the TEST SCORES worksheet. When you did this previously, you entered it in the first column and copied it into the remaining columns. This time you'll use

```
#1            1      #2     7                    8                  9
 5
 6 NAME                     TOTAL
 7 ================        =================
 8 ADAMS                    200 ******************************
 9 ANSEL                    215 ********************************
10 COPPER                   177 **************************
11 DUNN                     146 *********************
12 ETTENGER                 188 ***************************
13 JAMIESON                 205 *****************************
14 MCMURRY                  181 **************************
15 RADDER                   209 ******************************
16 SHAW                     164 ***********************
17                          ---------
18 AVERAGE SCORE            187.22
19
20 POSSIBLE SCORE           233
21
22
23
24
```

Figure 9-5. *Window #2 with data graphed*

another method. Move the cell pointer to R7C1, and with the Value command, enter the following function:

REPT("*",68)

The count 68 is the sum of all the column widths in the planning sheet. Press ENTER. Now, using the FORMAT cells command, format row 7 continuous through column 7, and a line of asterisks forms the separator.

If at any time you should decide to add or delete columns in the worksheet, you can increase or decrease the number of asterisks by using the Edit command and changing 68 to the appropriate value.

Saving a Worksheet as a Word-Processing File

There are instances when you will want to combine spreadsheet data from Multiplan with word-processing files. You can, of course, add a few sentences to a worksheet by making rows continuous; but for large reports it should be more convenient to use a word processor for the report text and Multiplan for the financial data, and then to combine the files to produce the final report.

Once a Multiplan file is saved with your word-processing file, you can edit the Multiplan text like word-processed text. This means you can add, delete, and reformat Multiplan data using all the tools of your word-processing program.

The Print/File command is used to move a worksheet to a word-processing file. The following examples use the WordStar word-processing program by MicroPro; other word-processing programs should work similarly.

Print/File

The Print/File command saves a copy of your worksheet on a disk in a format that is usable with a word-processing program like WordStar. Press Print and File, and Multiplan displays the following command line:

PRINT on file:

The message line asks you to enter a filename. You can enter any filename you choose, as long as the name conforms to the PC DOS requirements: eight letters or fewer for the filename and no more than three letters for the optional extension (separated from the filename by a period).

When the Print/File command is used, Multiplan does not assume that you are going to use the same filename that is displayed on the status line (as it does when you use the TRANSFER SAVE command). If you enter a name that is already on the disk, Multiplan will display the following message:

Overwrite existing file (Y \N) —

You then, of course, have the option of copying over the existing file or changing to a new filename. Remember that if you write this file over your current Multiplan file of the same name, you no longer have that worksheet for use with Multiplan. If you try to load a file that was saved with the Print/File command, the message line will display "File format error".

Saving your worksheet with the Print/File command allows it to be loaded by your word-processing program as a new file for editing or additions. If your word-processing program has the capability, your worksheet can also be "read" into an existing word-processing file at whatever position you wish.

Keep in mind that any selections you make with the PRINT MARGINS or PRINT OPTIONS commands will be retained when you use the Print/File command. When saving a file to be used with a word-processing program, set the width with the Margins command to a large enough value so that each row of the worksheet will be on a single line in the word-processing program. You can then rearrange the data if necessary. Note also that when you load a worksheet with the word-processing program, there will be several blank lines at the bottom of the worksheet. These can be removed with your word processor's delete command.

As an example, try transferring the TEST SCORES worksheet to a WordStar file.

Suppose you are the teacher and the principal requests a copy of your physics class list and the students' test scores. Press **P**rint and **O**ptions. You want to transfer only the data requested, so in the "area:" field enter the data shown in the following command line:

PRINT OPTIONS: area: R1C1:R20C7   setup:
formulas: Yes(No)   row-col numbers: Yes(No)

The remaining fields are correct, so press ENTER.

You are now back in the PRINT submenu. Press **M**argins. Change the values in each of the fields to match this command line:

PRINT MARGINS:left:0   top:0   print width:80
print length:54   page length:66

```
              B:PHY.WS   PAGE 1 LINE 1 COL 01
L----!----!----!----!----!----!----!----!----!----!----!--------R
                                                                          <
NAME              TEST1      TEST2      TEST3      TEST4        TOTAL      <
================================================================          <
ADAMS                54         30         65         51          200     <
ANSEL                61         31         71         52          215     <
COPPER               49         25         60         43          177     <
DUNN                 33         21         49         43          146     <
ETTENGER             52         23         66         47          188     <
JAMIESON             59         28         61         57          205     <
MCMURRY              53         29         57         42          181     <
RADDER               60         29         71         49          209     <
SHAW                 44         27         53         40          164     <
                 --------   --------   --------   --------     --------    <
AVERAGE SCORE     51.67      27.00      61.44      47.11       187.22      <
                                                                          <
POSSIBLE SCORE       65         33         80         55          233     <
                                                                          .
                                                                          .
                                                                          .
                                                                          .
 1HELP    2INDENT 3SET LM 4SET RM 5UNDLIN 6BLDFCE 7BEGBLK 8ENDBLK 9BEGFIL 10ENDFIL
```

Figure 9-6.   *Multiplan file loaded in WordStar*

```
To: Mr. Watkins
From: Walt Ettlin

      The information you requested for my second my second period
physics class is shown below.  If you have any questions
regarding individual students please let me know.


NAME                 TEST1      TEST2      TEST3      TEST4         TOTAL
============================================================================
ADAMS                   54         30         65         51           200
ANSEL                   61         31         71         52           215
COPPER                  49         25         60         43           177
DUNN                    33         21         49         43           146
ETTENGER                52         23         66         47           188
JAMIESON                59         28         61         57           205
MCMURRY                 53         29         57         42           181
RADDER                  60         29         71         49           209
SHAW                    44         27         53         40           164
                    --------   --------   --------   --------      --------
AVERAGE SCORE         51.67      27.00      61.44      47.11        187.22

POSSIBLE SCORE           65         33         80         55           233
```

Figure 9-7. *WordStar report with Multiplan data*

Zero is entered for the margins set in the "left:" and "top:" fields because those margins will be handled by WordStar. If you enter values in these fields, they will be added to the values that WordStar supplies. In the "print width:" field, 80 is used to allow complete rows to be printed on a single line. WordStar will override the values in the "paper length:" and "print length:" fields, so it doesn't matter what is entered there.

Press ENTER. You are again returned to the PRINT submenu. Press File. Type the name **PHY.WS** and press ENTER. With the file now saved on the disk, use the Quit command to quit Multiplan. You are now back in PC DOS.

Load WordStar. Press **D** to open a document file, and in answer to the message "NAME OF FILE TO EDIT?", type **PHY.WS**. The file loads and your screen looks like Figure 9-6.

Several blank lines are left at the end of your data, so use the Block Delete command to delete them. You can now edit the spreadsheet data like any document file. You are free to do whatever editing you please and, of course, add any message. See Figure 9-7 for an example.

Exercises

1. Graph the following data using the FORMAT cells command: 63, 45, 21, 72, 46, 38, 59, 52, 66.

2. Use the REPT function and the symbol # to graph the same data. Scale the graph so that it requires only two columns of standard width (that is, 20).

3. Use both of the previous methods to graph the decimal data given in "Graphing Decimals."

4. Display the graph from Exercise 3 and sort the data in descending order. Sort the data again in ascending order.

5. If you also work with a word-processing program, save the TEST SCORES worksheet with the Print/File command and load it with the word processor. Note the screen display and return to Multiplan. Next, change the field entries in the PRINT OPTIONS and PRINT MARGINS commands to see how the screen display changes when the program is again loaded with your word-processing program.

Working With Multiple Worksheets

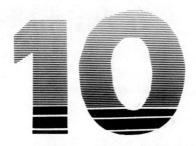

- A New Worksheet From an Old Worksheet
- The Options Command
- Tips on Speeding Up Large Worksheets
- Preparing for External Worksheets
- How to Use Supporting Worksheets
- Loading a Worksheet With External Links
- Properties of Linked Worksheets
- Severing Links
- Transferring Blocks With the Xternal Command

Commands

- Options
- GOTO NAME
- EXTERNAL COPY
- Xternal/List
- EXTERNAL USE

When the worksheet is large, Multiplan can take quite a long time to calculate (and recalculate) results. In this chapter you will explore what you can do to minimize these delays, and you will learn a technique that makes it easier to work with a large worksheet: you will learn to divide it into smaller sheets.

You will also be introduced to the use of the Xternal command. This command allows you to extract data from any number of worksheets and transfer it to a separate worksheet where a summary of the data can be compiled.

A New Worksheet From an Old Worksheet

Many types of worksheets, such as family budgets, business budgets, and expense accounts, are reproduced in nearly the same form each month. At the end of the year certain information will be extracted from each month's statement and compiled in a summary. Let's experiment with a couple of ways of reproducing worksheets and extracting and compiling information, so that you can pick the one best suited to your application.

Load the family budget program that you developed in Chapter 8. The status line should tell you that the computer's memory is 93% free. With only 7% used for January, you can easily add the other 11 months of the budget on this worksheet. First you'll add February and see what happens.

Rather than develop the February budget from scratch, you can copy the January budget and then use the Edit command to change the data. First place the cell pointer in R1C1; press Copy and then From. In the "cells:" field is R1C1; type a colon and press the END key. The cell pointer moves to R33C9. You do not have to copy the CODE table, so move the cell pointer to R33C7. Press TAB to move the edit cursor to the "to cells:" field. The cell pointer has automatically returned to R1C1, so press the PGDN key twice to move to R41C1. This command line should look like this:

COPY FROM cells: R1C1:R33C7   to cells: R41C1

Press ENTER. The January budget is now duplicated on the worksheet. To edit the second copy for February, you must do some reformatting, change the names and titles, and then enter the February data.

Scroll the screen to display rows 41 through 60. As you can see, the rows that were formatted continuous in the January budget need to be formatted continuous for February. Do this to rows 42 and 43 and to row 53 (and only to the columns necessary). In line 43 use the Edit command to change JANUARY to FEBRUARY. Now use the Name command to change all the names for this worksheet, and of course, be sure to correct the "to refer to:" field so that the cell assignments are appropriate for this portion of the worksheet. You have to change the names TOTAL1 to TOTAL2, INCOME1 to INCOME2, and AMOUNT1 to AMOUNT2. Also adjust the formulas that require the new names.

Many of the companies to which you issue checks will be the same in both months. There will be some changes that you'll take care of shortly, but for now leave the company names and codes on the budget, and blank the date, check, amount, and interest data. For you to do this, the command line should read

BLANK: R54C3:R71C7

Press ENTER.

The entire worksheet is shown in Figure 10-1. Because you changed the name assignments and formulas for use in the February section, January's data will not be affected as you enter the new data.

```
              1           2          3        4         5         6          7
 1
 2                     AMES FAMILY MONTHLY BILLS
 3                            JANUARY 84
 4
 5         INCOME:        BEG. BAL.             232.80
 6                        J. AIMS              1153.87
 7                        R. AIMS              1456.77
 8                                             ----------
 9                        TOTAL                2843.44
10
11                                                            INTEREST
12  COMPANY             CODE      DATE   CHECK    AMOUNT       PAID    EARNED
13  ********************************************************************************
14  TELEPHONE             0      01/01    131      23.45
15  GAS & ELECTRIC        0      01/01    132     108.88
16  WATER                 0      01/01    133       8.75
17  GARBAGE               0      01/01    134      12.50
18  TV CABLE              0      01/01    135      18.50
19  VISA                  1      01/01    136     212.56      17.45
20  1st NATIONAL          2      01/01    137     407.96     397.31
21  ALLSTATE (CAR)        5      01/01    138     243.21
22  BLUE CROSS            4      01/01    139     211.34
23  MACY'S                1      01/01    140      89.03       5.33
24  SEARS                 1      01/01    141     156.77       8.93
25  SHELL OIL             1      01/01    142      93.46
26  SAFEWAY               7      01/02    144      95.79
27  SAFEWAY               7      01/09    145      89.71
28  CLEANERS              8      01/09    146      27.34
29  SAFEWAY               7      01/16    147      93.12
30  SAFEWAY               7      01/23    148      99.93
31  SAVINGS               6      01/01    143     450.00              34.98
32                                               ----------
33                                               2442.30
34
35
36
37
38
39
40
41
42                    AMES FAMILY MONTHLY BILLS
43                           FEBRUARY 84
44
45         INCOME:        BEG. BAL.             232.80
46                        J. AIMS              1153.87
47                        R. AIMS              1456.77
48                                             ----------
49                        TOTAL                2843.44
50
51                                                            INTEREST
52  COMPANY             CODE      DATE   CHECK    AMOUNT       PAID    EARNED
53  ********************************************************************************
54  TELEPHONE             0
55  GAS & ELECTRIC        0
56  WATER                 0
57  GARBAGE               0
58  TV CABLE              0
59  VISA                  1
```

Figure 10-1. *Family budget for January and February*

```
60  1st NATIONAL       2
61  ALLSTATE (CAR)     5
62  BLUE CROSS         4
63  MACY'S             1
64  SEARS              1
65  SHELL OIL          1
66  SAFEWAY            7
67  SAFEWAY            7
68  CLEANERS           8
69  SAFEWAY            7
70  SAFEWAY            7
71  SAVINGS            6
```

Figure 10-1. *Family budget for January and February (continued)*

The Options Command

As you have seen whenever a calculation is performed, Multiplan typically displays results immediately. However, as the filled-in area of a worksheet becomes larger, this calculation and display process becomes time-consuming. For such circumstances Multiplan supplies a handy feature that allows you to delay the calculation routine until all data is entered in a worksheet, and then to perform all calculations and display the results at once. You turn off automatic recalculation by using the Options command.

You'll use this command to see how recalculation is delayed while you enter the February data. First press **O**ptions, and the command line displays

OPTIONS recalc: <u>Yes</u> No   mute: Yes (No)
            iteration: Yes (No)   completion test at:

The "recalc:" field controls automatic recalculation. When the field is set to Yes, recalculation takes place automatically every time data is entered into a cell; when it is set to No, recalculation is not automatic and will not be performed until you instruct Multiplan to do it. (For your information, the "mute:" field allows you to control the "bell" that rings when you give Multiplan an illegal command; you can leave it on (No, its default setting) or turn it off (Yes) as you prefer. You will learn about the uses of the "iteration:" and "completion test at:" fields in Chapter 13.) In the "recalc:" field, press **N** or the space bar to highlight No. The other fields remain the same, so press ENTER.

Now when you enter the data for the February budget, recalculation in the cells containing formulas will not occur automatically. When you are ready to recalculate a worksheet, you can press the F4 key.

Prepare to enter the February data by scrolling your screen to display rows 52 through 71. Move the cell pointer to row 54 and divide the screen into two horizontal windows. February's data is shown in Table 10-1. The ending balance of January should be entered as the beginning balance of February.

To change the list of company names in column 1, use the Insert and Delete commands as necessary. When you have entered all the data for February, press F4. The calculations are performed throughout the entire worksheet, and the results are displayed. The February section of the worksheet appears in Figure 10-2.

Return the worksheet now to the automatic recalculation option. To request it, press **O**ptions and then **Y**es in the "recalc:" field. Press ENTER.

Income: J. AMES 1153.87
　　　　　 R. AMES 1456.77

COMPANY	CODE	DATE	CHECK	AMOUNT	INTEREST PAID	EARNED
TELEPHONE	0	02/01	144	33.74		
GAS & ELECTRIC	0	02/01	145	112.63		
WATER	0	02/01	146	8.01		
GARBAGE	0	02/01	147	12.50		
TV CABLE	0	02/01	148	18.50		
VISA	1	02/01	149	350.00	23.20	
1st NATIONAL	2	02/01	150	407.96	396.87	
ALLSTATE (CAR)	5	02/01	151	243.21		
BLUE CROSS	4	02/01	152	211.34		
MACY'S	1	02/01	153	196.91	6.50	
SHELL OIL	1	02/01	154	102.05	4.20	
SAFEWAY	7	02/01	155	103.76		
SAFEWAY	7	02/11	156	94.23		
BAKERY	8	02/11	157	12.59		
SAFEWAY	7	02/18	158	90.11		
SAFEWAY	7	02/25	159	95.43		
CASH	8	02/25	160	75.00		
SAVINGS	6	02/25	161	550.00		38.01

Table 10-1.   *February Data for Family Budget*

```
#1          1        2        3      4      5          6        7
41
42                     AMES FAMILY MONTHLY BILLS
43                          FEBRUARY 84
44
45          INCOME:        BEG. BAL.        401.14
46                         J. AIMS         1153.87
47                         R. AIMS         1456.77
48                                        ----------
49                         TOTAL           3011.78
50
51                                                          INTEREST
52  COMPANY            CODE     DATE   CHECK   AMOUNT      PAID   EARNED
53  ******************************************************************
54  TELEPHONE           0      02/01   144      33.74
55  GAS & ELECTRIC      0      02/01   145     112.63
56  WATER               0      02/01   146       8.01
57  GARBAGE             0      02/01   147      12.50
58  TV CABLE            0      02/01   148      18.5
59  VISA                1      02/01   149     350.00      23.20
60  1st NATIONAL        2      02/01   150     407.96     396.87
61  ALLSTATE (CAR)      5      02/01   151     243.21
62  BLUE CROSS          4      02/01   152     211.34
63  MACY'S              1      02/01   153     196.91       6.50
64  SHELL OIL           1      02/01   154     102.05       4.20
65  SAFEWAY             7      02/01   155     103.76
66  SAFEWAY             7      02/11   156      94.23
67  BAKERY              8      02/11   157      12.59
68  SAFEWAY             7      02/18   158      90.11
69  SAFEWAY             7      02/25   159      95.43
70  CASH                8      02/25   160      75.00
71  SAVINGS             6      02/25   161     550.00               38.01
72                                           ----------  --------  --------
73                                            2717.97     430.77    38.01
74
75
76  END BALANCE
77          293.81
```

Figure 10-2. *February budget calculations*

Tips on Speeding Up Large Worksheets

You now have a fairly large worksheet, but the computer's memory is still 89%
free. As would be expected when the size of a worksheet is nearly doubled, it
takes more time to move from one section of the sheet to another, because more
memory is in use. For the same reason, when you enter new information into this
worksheet, recalculation takes longer. Follow these guidelines for minimizing
delays when worksheets become large:

1. Keep your worksheets as compact as possible. Avoid unnecessary columns
   and rows between sections of the worksheet.

2. If you no longer need a section of your worksheet, use the Delete command, rather than the Blank command, to delete the rows and columns.

3. Use continuous format for rows only where necessary. For example, if you need to use the Cont command only for columns 4, 5, and 6 in row 5, do not apply it to the complete row.

4. Use functions and operators only for the range necessary. For example, if you wish to SUM a group of numbers in column 5, rows 6 through 12, use the formula SUM(R6:12C5) rather than SUM(C5).

5. Turn off the automatic recalculation option when entering data into a large worksheet. When the entries are complete, press F4 to recalculate the worksheet all at once.

If you haven't already turned off automatic recalculation, try this now with the Options command: Press **O**ptions, and in the "recalc:" field press **N**o; then press ENTER. Scroll the worksheet to display rows 54 through 73 and columns 1 through 7. Enter some numbers (as values, not Alpha entries) in column 7 and notice that the total in R73C7 does not change. Press F4 to recalculate, and the sum for INTEREST EARNED immediately reflects the correct amount.

6. Divide your worksheet at logical points into two or more smaller worksheets. This is not the same thing as dividing the worksheet into windows. With additional worksheets, you can use the Xternal command to extract data and summarize it on another worksheet. You'll learn to do this later in the chapter.

Goto/Name

When worksheets become large, it is convenient to use the GOTO name command to move quickly from one section to another. For example, you can do this with the family budget worksheet, which has two major sections, the January and February budgets.

The first step is to assign a name to each section. It makes no difference what names you assign as long as they have some meaning to you. In this instance, use the name JAN for the January budget and FEB for the February budget. The cell to which the name is assigned is also up to you, but it should be near the central work area of the section you are moving to. The first item in the list of companies is a reasonable choice.

Try this now. Move the cell pointer over TELEPHONE in R54C1. Press **N**ame and replace TELEPHONE in the "define name:" field by typing in **FEB** as the cell name. The entry in the "to refer to:" field is correct, so press ENTER. Now move the cell pointer over TELEPHONE in R14C1. Again press **N**ame and type the name **JAN.** The "to refer to:" field is again correct, so press ENTER.

A third section of this worksheet that you could name is the code table. To name it, place the cell pointer over CODE, in R1C9, and press **N**ame. Use CODE for the name and have it refer to its actual position, R1C9.

Now try moving to the various sections of the worksheet with the GOTO name command. Press **G**oto and ENTER for Name. The command line displays the following:

GOTO name:

Press the right arrow key until the name FEB comes up in the "name:" field. Press ENTER. You immediately move to the cell assigned the name FEB. Try moving to other sections of the worksheet with the newly assigned names.

Of course you can also move to any of the other sections that have names, such as INCOME1, INCOME2, and so on. If the name to go to refers to a block, the cell pointer moves to the cell in the upper-left corner of that block.

Moving around a large worksheet can become time-consuming even when you're using the GOTO name command. You still have plenty of room to add the March budget, but let's consider an alternative to increasing the size of this worksheet.

Preparing for External Worksheets

One alternative to building one very large annual family budget worksheet is to use a separate worksheet for each month and then use the Xternal command to extract information from each month's budget and compile it into a year-end summary worksheet.

In a year-end summary of their finances, the Ames family may be interested in the following data from each monthly budget: total income, total expenses, interest paid and earned, and medical expenses. You will be setting up a separate worksheet for each month, and you'll have to be sure the necessary data is labeled in these categories so that it can be transferred to the summary sheet. These worksheets will become *support* worksheets for the summary sheet.

You will create another worksheet that contains the budget summary information. It will be the *active* worksheet, that is, the worksheet that is loaded in memory and displayed on the screen. It will also contain the commands for extracting data from the support worksheet files. See Figure 10-3 for a diagram of how the worksheets are related.

You now have two major tasks: first, to create the three separate monthly budgets; and second, to plan and create the summary worksheet that will contain the yearly data. To create the three monthly budgets, you will split the

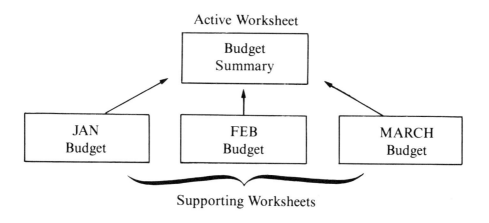

Figure 10-3.   *The active worksheet and supporting worksheets*

January and February budgets into two separate files and then create the March budget.

The January and February files will be named BUDJAN.C10 and BUD-FEB.C10. Follow these steps to create the two files:

1. Save BUDGET.C8, the current worksheet, under the name BUDJAN.C10.
2. Save it again under the name BUDFEB.C10.
3. Clear the screen.
4. Load BUDJAN.C10.
5. With the Delete command erase the section containing the February budget, R41C1:R77C7. Be sure to use Delete and not Blank.
6. Save BUDJAN.C10.
7. Load BUDFEB.C10.
8. Delete the section containing the January budget, R1C1:R40C7.
9. Save BUDFEB.C10.

You now have two Multiplan files, each containing one month's budget.

The easiest way to create the March budget is to edit the February budget that is currently displayed. After editing it for March data, you will save it using the name BUDMAR.C10.

Just as you did for February, correct the formulas and titles to produce the March budget. When assigning names to it, leave off the digit 3: Monthly indicators are no longer necessary since there is a separate worksheet for each month. Enter the data for March provided in Table 10-2. When complete, your March budget should appear as shown in Figure 10-4. Save the worksheet with the filename BUDMAR.C10, and then clear the screen.

Now you are ready for the second task: planning and entering the BUDGET SUMMARY worksheet. Figure 10-5 shows the planning sheet for the worksheet.

Set up the worksheet. When complete, the screen should look like Figure 10-6. When you use this worksheet, you will use the filname BUDSUM.C10. The current worksheet will be referred to by that name in the following discussion.

How to Use Supporting Worksheets

With your summary worksheet complete, let's transfer the data from the January budget to it. To transfer data from a supporting worksheet to the active worksheet, you use the Xternal command and Copy subcommand. With these commands you can designate the *source* cell (from which you will extract data on the supporting worksheets) in either of two ways: by absolute reference or by Name reference.

Income: J. AMES 1153.87
R. AMES 1456.77

COMPANY	CODE	DATE	CHECK	AMOUNT	INTEREST PAID	EARNED
TELEPHONE	0	03/03	162	23.40		
GAS & ELECTRIC	0	03/03	163	103.55		
WATER	0	03/03	164	11.03		
GARBAGE	0	03/03	165	12.50		
TV CABLE	0	03/03	167	18.50		
VISA	1	03/03	168	215.33	19.87	
1st NATIONAL	2	03/03	169	407.96	396.37	
BLUE CROSS	4	03/03	171	211.34		
MACY'S	1	02/01	172	78.30		
SHELL OIL	1	03/03	173	88.43	3.51	
SAFEWAY	7	03/03	174	94.01		
LUCKY	7	03/10	175	96.30		
BAKERY	8	03/10	176	17.20		
CASH	7	03/17	177	50.00		
SAFEWAY	7	03/17	178	88.56		
SAFEWAY	6	03/24	180	89.47		
MEDICAL (DRUGS)	4	03/24	181	38.14		
SAFEWAY	7	03/31	182	103.22		
BAKERY	8	03/31	183	11.40		
SAVINGS	6	03/31	184	800.00		44.31

Table 10-2.   *March Data for Family Budget*

Xternal/Copy

To begin, place the cell pointer in R8C2. Press **X**ternal, and the command line displays the following:

EXTERNAL: Copy List Use

Copy is the subcommand that allows you to use data from the supporting

	1	2	3	4	5	6	7
1							
2		AMES FAMILY MONTHLY BILLS					
3			MARCH 84				
4							
5	INCOME:		BEG. BAL.		293.81		
6			J. AMES		1241.25		
7			R. AMES		1456.77		
8					----------		
9			TOTAL		2991.83		
10						INTEREST	
11						PAID	EARNED
12	COMPANY	CODE	DATE	CHECK	AMOUNT		
13	**						
14	TELEPHONE	0	03/03	162	23.40		
15	GAS & ELECTRIC	0	03/03	163	103.55		
16	WATER	0	03/03	164	11.03		
17	GARBAGE	0	03/03	165	12.50		
18	TV CABLE	0	03/03	167	18.50		
19	VISA	1	03/03	168	215.33	19.87	
20	1st NATIONAL	2	03/03	169	407.96	396.37	
21	BLUE CROSS	4	03/03	171	211.34		
22	MACY'S	1	03/03	172	78.30		
23	SHELL OIL	1	03/03	173	88.43	3.51	
24	SAFEWAY	7	03/03	174	94.01		
25	LUCKY	7	03/10	175	96.30		
26	BAKERY	8	03/10	176	17.20		
27	CASH	7	03/17	177	50.00		
28	SAFEWAY	7	03/17	178	88.56		
29	SAFEWAY	6	03/24	180	89.47		
30	MEDICAL (DRUGS)	4	03/24	181	38.14		
31	SAFEWAY	7	03/31	182	103.22		
32	BAKERY	8	03/31	183	11.40		
33	SAVINGS	6	03/31	184	800.00		44.31
34					---------	--------	--------
35					2558.64	419.75	44.31
36							
37							
38	END BALANCE						
39	$433.19						

Figure 10-4.   *March budget*

worksheets, so press ENTER to display this command line:

EXTERNAL COPY from sheet: name:
                         to: R8C2   linked: (Yes)No

In the first field, "from sheet:", enter the filename BUDJAN.C10, the source sheet for the data. Press TAB to move to the "name:" field. You want the total income, so, using absolute reference, type **R9C5** (this is the cell on the January budget worksheet that contains the total income). Press TAB to move the edit cursor to the "to:" field. Since your cell pointer was in R8C2 when you pressed

```
                                BUDGET  SUMMARY

          (d)          (d)         (d)        (d)       (d)        (d)
           1            2           3          4         5          6
    1                              AMES  FAMILY                              (Cont.)
    2                              BUDGET  SUMMARY
    3                                 1984
    4
    5                                              INTEREST
    6  MONTH         (INCOME     EXPENSE       PAID     EARNED     MEDICAL) (Rt. Just.)
    7  =========================================================================== (Separator =)
    8  JANUARY
    9  FEBRUARY                       FIX 2 [R8C2:R13C6]
   10  MARCH
   11
   12
   13         _____    _____    _____   _____   _____
   14


          NAMES:     INCOME     R7:12C2
                     EXPENSE    R7:12C3
                     PAID       R7:12C4
                     EARNED     R7:12C5
                     MEDICAL    R7:12C6

          FORMULAS:  REPT("=",60)        R7C1
                     SUM(INCOME)         R13C2
                     SUM(EXPENSE)        R13C3
                     SUM(PAID)           R13C4
                     SUM(EARNED)         R13C5
                     SUM(MEDICAL)        R13C6
```

Figure 10-5. *Budget summary planning sheet*

Xternal, the reference is correct. Press TAB to move to the "linked:" field and press **No**. The command line displays

EXTERNAL COPY from sheet: BUDJAN.C10   name: R9C5
                       to: R8C2   linked: Yes(No)

Press ENTER and Multiplan copies the data from the January budget file to the active worksheet, BUDSUM.C10, and displays it on the screen. Note that the source file must be on the same disk as the active worksheet.

Use the SUM function to determine the sum for INTEREST PAID and INTEREST EARNED and then follow the procedure just described to transfer the information from your *support worksheet*, BUDJAN.C10, for EXPENSE, INTEREST PAID, and INTEREST EARNED to the active sheet. Do not transfer the data for MEDICAL; you will be shown a method of doing this in the next chapter. If all works correctly, your screen should look like Figure 10-7.

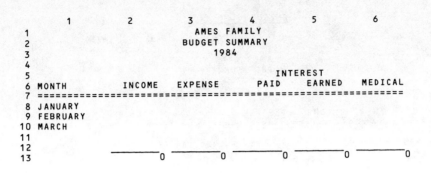

```
            1           2           3           4           5           6
                                            AMES FAMILY
 1
 2                                         BUDGET SUMMARY
 3                                             1984
 4
 5                                                     INTEREST
 6  MONTH            INCOME    EXPENSE        PAID    EARNED    MEDICAL
 7  ================================================================
 8  JANUARY
 9  FEBRUARY
10  MARCH
11
12
13  _____     0 _____ 0 _____ 0 _____ 0 _____ 0
```

Figure 10-6.   *The BUDGET SUMMARY worksheet*

```
            1           2           3           4           5           6
                                            AMES FAMILY
 1
 2                                         BUDGET SUMMARY
 3                                             1984
 4
 5                                                     INTEREST
 6  MONTH            INCOME    EXPENSE        PAID    EARNED    MEDICAL
 7  ================================================================
 8  JANUARY         2843.44    2442.30      429.02     34.98
 9  FEBRUARY
10  MARCH
11
12
13                  2843.44    2442.3       429.02     34.98              0
```

Figure 10-7.   *Summary worksheet with January data*

You are going to transfer the data from the February worksheet as well. But this time you will reference cells using Name references and you will "link" the worksheets.

Now save your summary worksheet, using the name BUDSUM.C10, and load the February worksheet, BUDFEB.C10. Next, with the Name command, assign the following names to the data you want to transfer to the specified cells: INCOME to R9C5, EXPENSE to R33C5, INTPD (for "interest paid") to

R33C6, and INTERN (for "interest earned") to R33C7. (These cell numbers will be correct only if you deleted *exactly* 40 lines to create the final form of BUDFEB.C10, moving the data in row 73 to row 33.) Save the worksheet using the same name, BUDFEB.C10.

Reload BUDSUM.C10. Move the cell pointer to R9C2 and press **X**ternal and **C**opy. In the "from sheet:" field enter BUDFEB.C10 and press TAB. In the "name:" field enter INCOME. The reference in the "to:" field is correct. In the "linked:" field leave Yes in parentheses. Press ENTER.

Use the same procedure to transfer the data in the columns for EXPENSE, INTEREST PAID, and INTEREST EARNED. Notice that now, when you select the Xternal command, the "name:" field contains BUDFEB.C10. This is the default entry because it was given in your last entry, in which you kept the Yes option in the "linked:" field.

Again save BUDSUM.C10. Load the March budget worksheet, BUD-MAR.C10, and assign names to the cells that you want transferred. Since the names will be on a different worksheet, you can assign the same ones you used for the February sheet. Save BUDMAR.C10 and load the summary sheet again. Using the Xternal copy command, copy the data to the summary worksheet. With the three months' data, your screen should look the same as Figure 10-8.

As always, you should be aware of the information that is available to you on the status line. Move the cell pointer to R8C3 and notice that the value in that cell is printed on the status line as you would expect. Move the cell pointer to the next row down, to R9C3. Instead of displaying the value in cell R9C3, the status line displays [BUDFEB.C10 EXPENSE]—the filename of the worksheet the

```
#1        1          2          3         4        5        6        7
 1                              AMES  FAMILY
 2                              BUDGET  SUMMARY
 3                                 1984
 4
 5                                                INTEREST
 6  MONTH         INCOME     EXPENSE      PAID    EARNED    MEDICAL
 7  ==========================================================
 8  JANUARY       2843.44    2442.30    429.02    34.98
 9  FEBRUARY      3011.78    2717.97    430.77    38.01
10  MARCH         2991.83    2558.64    419.75    44.31
11
12              _____   _____   _____   _____          ____
13               8847.05    7718.91    1279.54    117.3            0
14
15
```

Figure 10-8. *Summary worksheet with three months' data*

data came from (BUDFEB.C10) and the name that applies to that data (EXPENSE). This information is supplied for this cell because the February budget sheet is *linked* to the active worksheet, and the active worksheet will remember the reference rather than just accept the value. Data from the January budget was not linked to the BUDGET SUMMARY worksheet, and so no new values will be extracted from that worksheet.

A couple of additional points are worth noting. First, when extracting data from any worksheet, you can use either absolute or name references. Second, if the data being transferred to an active worksheet comes from more than one source cell in a worksheet, the "linked:" field for each cell can be set independently of the others; one or more might be set Yes and one or more set No. Third, you can transfer not only single cells of data, but also blocks of data, as will be discussed later in this chapter.

Loading a Worksheet With External Links

When a worksheet has *external links* —that is, when you have set a "linked:" field in the EXTERNAL command line to Yes—every time you load that worksheet the data is extracted from the supporting sheets to the active sheet. To see what happens, save the BUDGET SUMMARY sheet, BUDSUM.C10, and then reload it. You will notice two things. First, it takes a little longer to load; second, the message line tells you what data is being copied from the supporting sheets (for example, "Copying: BUDFEB.C10 INCOME"). Since the January data is not linked to the summary sheet, it is not extracted when the summary sheet is reloaded (although the summary sheet retains the values originally extracted). If January totals change, the BUDGET SUMMARY will not automatically be adjusted.

The advantage of linking two sheets, then, is that if data changes in the supporting worksheets, the active worksheet is automatically updated. For example, if you changed data in the February budget, the monthly totals in that worksheet would change, and the correct totals would automatically be transferred to the summary worksheet the next time BUDSUM.C10 was loaded. The disadvantage of linking two sheets is the increased time that it takes to load the active sheet.

Xternal/List

Now that you have supporting sheets linked to BUDSUM.C10, let's examine the Xternal/List command. Press Xternal, and from the EXTERNAL command line, press **List**. Your screen looks like Figure 10-9.

The screen displays the names of the supporting worksheets that are linked to BUDSUM.C10. The filename of the January sheet is not displayed, since no link was established between it and the active sheet. No sheets depend on BUD-SUM.C10, but some could. For example, you might have a worksheet titled BUDMAST, for "budget master," that contains all the information necessary for calculating taxes. BUDMAST would extract information from the family BUDGET SUMMARY, BUDSUM.C10, as well as from worksheets containing information on travel and other business expenses.

No more than eight worksheets can support a given worksheet at one time. However, there is no limit to the number of sheets that can depend on a given sheet.

At the bottom of your screen the message "Press any key to redraw screen" is displayed. Press the space bar (or any key) to return to the BUDGET SUM-MARY worksheet.

To see all of the worksheet connections, use the FORMAT OPTIONS command; press **Format** and **Options**. Move the edit cursor to the "formulas:" field and press **Yes**. Press ENTER and your screen looks like Figure 10-10.

Here you can see the linked cells and their worksheet names displayed as formulas.

```
Sheets supporting BUDSUM.C10

BUDFEB.C10
BUDMAR.C10


No sheets depend on BUDSUM.C10
```

```
Press any key to redraw screen
R10C5     [BUDMAR.C10 INTER]              98% Free   NL   Multiplan: BUDSUM.C10
```

Figure 10-9.   *Screen after pressing Xternal and List*

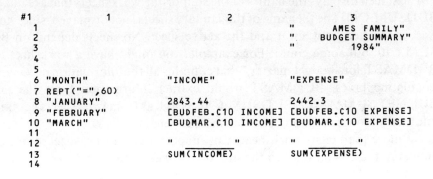

```
#1              1                 2                    3
 1                                        "      AMES  FAMILY"
 2                                        "    BUDGET  SUMMARY"
 3                                        "         1984"
 4
 5
 6  "MONTH"           "INCOME"          "EXPENSE"
 7  REPT("=",60)
 8  "JANUARY"         2843.44           2442.3
 9  "FEBRUARY"        [BUDFEB.C10 INCOME]   [BUDFEB.C10 EXPENSE]
10  "MARCH"           [BUDMAR.C10 INCOME]   [BUDMAR.C10 EXPENSE]
11
12                    "        "         "          "
13                    SUM(INCOME)       SUM(EXPENSE)
14
```

Figure 10-10. *The active worksheet displaying linked cells and worksheet names as formulas*

Properties of Linked Worksheets

There are several important points to keep in mind when working with linked worksheets:

1. All data transferred from the supporting sheet to the active sheet is locked on the active sheet. The Lock command will not unlock these cells. The only way to unlock them is to sever the link between the support sheet and the active sheet (see "Severing Links").
2. If the data transferred to the active sheet was generated by a formula, only the data is transferred and not the formula.
3. The destination cell on the active worksheet must be blank. Multiplan will not overwrite a cell containing data. Likewise, if a block of information is being transferred, the entire block must be blank on the active sheet. If you attempt to copy data into an occupied cell, the message line will display "Cannot copy into nonblank cell."
4. When a block of data is transferred, the block on the active sheet will be the same size and shape as the block on the support
5. If a particular cell in a support sheet is linked to the active sheet, you can copy the data from that cell to only one destination on the active worksheet. (If there is no link, you can copy the contents of the cell to as many cells in the active worksheet as you like.) If you wish to change the destination, use the EXTERNAL COPY command to send the data to the new destination, but the cell that contained the data previously will be blanked.

6. You press the right arrow and left arrow keys to step through the names in the "from sheet:" field and the absolute references or names in the "name:" field.

Severing Links

The following procedure is used to sever the links between the active worksheet and the supporting worksheets. But first use the FORMAT OPTIONS command and enter a **Y** in the "formulas:" field to display the existing links on your screen. Do this now by displaying the formulas for the BUDGET SUMMARY worksheet for rows 1 through 20 and columns 1 through 3.

Move the cell pointer to R9C2 and press **X**ternal and **C**opy. In the "from sheet:" field, press the right arrow key to obtain the filename BUDFEB.C10. Then press the TAB key to move to the "name:" field. Again press the right arrow key to obtain the name INCOME. Press the TAB key to move to the "to:" field and press DEL to delete the reference. In the "linked:" field the word Yes must be in parentheses. (It is.) The command line displays

EXTERNAL COPY: from sheet: BUDFEB.C10   name: INCOME
        to: linked: (Yes)No

Press ENTER. The entry for the February income in R9C2 is now blank. To sever the connection completely between the active sheet and a supporting sheet, you must break all links to all cells. The same procedure must be used to break the links for the EXPENSE, INTEREST PAID, and INTEREST EARNED cells.

Break the remaining links to the February budget worksheet and use the Xternal/List command to verify that it is not shown in the list of "Sheets supporting BUDSUM.C10".

Transferring Blocks With the Xternal Command

So far you have transferred data only from individual cells of the support sheet to the active sheet. Now you will try transferring a block of data. Load the worksheet BUDJAN.C10 and assign the name CODE to cover the data in the table. The command line will display the following:

NAME: define name:CODE   to refer to:R1C9:R10C9

Press ENTER and then save the worksheet. Load the BUDFEB.C10 worksheet.

Scroll the worksheet so it displays rows 1 through 20 and columns 4 through 10. Place the cell pointer in R1C9. Press **X**ternal and **C**opy. In the "from sheet:" field type **BUDJAN.C10**. Press TAB, and in the "name:" field type **CODE**. The "to:" field and the "linked:" field are correct, so press ENTER. Format the cells containing the code table to be continuous. You now have a usable code reference table in your February worksheet. Your screen looks like Figure 10-11.

You will find that transferring blocks of data will come in handy in many of the worksheets you design.

Xternal/Use

The final Xternal command, EXTERNAL USE, allows you to substitute one supporting sheet for another. Before you learn how to use this command, save your current worksheet and load the January budget worksheet.

In the January worksheet the name INCOME1 is assigned to R9C5. Keep this name and assignment, but also assign the name INCOME to R9C5. The name INCOME is already assigned to the total income for the February and March worksheets, so now INCOME is assigned to this data in all three worksheets.

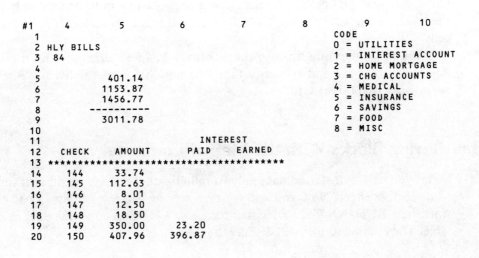

Figure 10-11.   *February with the code table entered by EXTERNAL COPY*

Save the January worksheet and use TRANSFER CLEAR to clear the screen.

Load the BUDGET SUMMARY, BUDSUM.C10. Move the cell pointer to R1C1, and with the Alpha command, enter the word INCOME. Move the cell pointer to R1C2—you're going to establish a link between this worksheet and the January budget. Press **X**ternal and **C**opy. In the "from sheet:" field enter BUDJAN.C10. Press TAB to move to the "name:" field. Type **INCOME**. The "to:" field and "linked:" field are correct, so press ENTER. The total income of the Ames family in January, 2843.44, appears in the active cell. Now press **X**ternal and **U**se; you are now presented with the following command line:

EXTERNAL USE filename: instead of: BUDJAN.C10.

In the "filename:" field type the name **BUDFEB.C10**. Now examine the command line. It tells you that you are going to use the budget sheet for February instead of the one for January. The information extracted from the February budget will be printed in R1C2. Press ENTER. You have not established any links between the February budget worksheet and the active sheet, but you have substituted it for the January sheet for which you did have links. The total income of the Ames family in February, 3011.78, appears in R1C2. Notice that the status line continues to refer to the January budget. Also note that the destination cell, R1C2, was not blank as is required when the EXTERNAL COPY command is used to transfer data between linked worksheets.

Using this single link and this example worksheet, you can examine the income for the March budget or for any other month of the year for which you have worksheets. You may also use this command to read the January income by placing BUDJAN.C10 in the "filename:" field and keeping BUDJAN.C10 in the "instead of:" field.

You have now worked with all of Multiplan's commands, most of its subcommands, and a few of its functions. You will need the information presented in Chapters 1 through 10 in order to design and use worksheets efficiently. In the final four chapters of this book, you will be introduced to numerous functions from which you can select the ones most helpful in designing worksheets suited to your needs. The more tools you have available, the more efficient your design of worksheets will become.

Exercises

1. Load the January budget program, and format rows 1 through 40 to be continuous for all 63 columns. Scroll the screen, both horizontally and vertically. Then change the continuous format to cover only columns 1 through 10 by setting the block R1C11:R40C63 to Def in the "format code:" field, and note the marked improvement in speed.

2. Load the TEST SCORES worksheet and insert a column for homework scores before the "dummy" column. With the Options command turn "recalc" off and enter data you make up. Blank the column and enter the data again with "recalc" on to note the difference.

3. Use the EXTERNAL COPY command to transfer the CODE and AMOUNT columns from the three monthly budget worksheets to columns 2 and 3 of a new worksheet.

	CODE	AMOUNT
codes JAN	0 0 . . .	23.45 108.88 . . .
codes FEB	0 0 . . .	33.74 112.63 . . .
codes MARCH	0 0 . . .	23.40 103.55 . . .

4. Use the Sort command to sort the data by CODE in the worksheet you created in Exercise 3.

5. Sever the links between BUDSUM.C10 and the March budget worksheet.

Working
With Functions

- The General Format of a Function
- The COLUMN and ROW Functions
- The DOLLAR, FIXED, and VALUE
  Functions
- The ROUND Function
- The MAX, MIN, and STDEV Functions
- Using Functions as Arguments
- The LEN, MID, and INT Functions
- The LOOKUP Function

Functions

- COLUMN
- ROW
- DOLLAR
- FIXED
- VALUE
- ROUND
- MAX
- MIN
- STDEV
- LEN
- MID
- INT
- LOOKUP

You will be introduced to the use of the remaining Multiplan functions in this and the following chapters (you've already learned several functions in Chapters 7 and 8). You may never use all of them, but each function is another tool at your disposal when you are designing a worksheet. Some are easy to use and others can be challenging. You will learn their appropriate format through experience with simple examples.

Many of the functions are used individually but can also be used in combination with other functions, and some functions are used almost exclusively with others. The number of combinations is unlimited. A few examples of using combined functions are included to acquaint you with the possibilities available in Multiplan. They may seem difficult at first, but keep in mind that only time and experience will give you the background you need to make full use of Multiplan's functions.

The General Format of a Function

Before you go any further in this discussion of functions, let's consider their general structure. First you must use the Value command to enter a function. Second, whether you type them in caps or lowercase letters, functions always display in capital letters — for example, SUM. Third, most functions are followed by an *argument* or a set of arguments enclosed in parentheses — for example, SUM(List). The arguments provide the data required to execute the function; in the SUM function, for example, the single argument, List, references the range or ranges of cells to be added. Fourth, every function, whether it has an argument or not, is followed by a set of parentheses — for example, ROW().

Functions always determine a value depending on the argument(s) you supply. This value is referred to as the *value returned*. The value returned is not always a numeric value. For example, REPT("=",8) returns eight equals signs; this result is referred to as a *text value*.

You have been introduced to three function arguments so far:

List   (for listing numbers)
T   (for text)
Count   (for how many)

In the function REPT("=",8), two of these arguments are used: the T argument, where T = "="; and the Count argument, where Count = 8. The List argument was used with the functions SUM, AVERAGE, and COUNT in Chapter 7. As new functions are introduced, you'll be introduced to the arguments that apply to each.

As you move from function to function and practice using them in examples, you will not be instructed to save the worksheets unless they will be used later. If you wish to save any for reference, be sure to do so before you clear the screen for the next example.

The COLUMN and ROW Functions

The COLUMN and ROW functions have no arguments, but as mentioned, still require parentheses, since they identify the function word, COLUMN or ROW, to Multiplan. When you use the COLUMN function in a formula, it returns the value of the column that the cell pointer is in when the function is used. Similarly, the ROW function returns the row number that the cell pointer is in.

COLUMN

The format of the COLUMN function is COLUMN(). To see its use, move the cell pointer to R3C4. Select the Value command and type **COLUMN()**. The command line displays

VALUE: COLUMN()

Press ENTER and the number 4 appears in R3C4. As always, the status line displays the formula that produced this result; in this case, it displays the function COLUMN.

One practical use for the COLUMN function is in constructing a calendar. Try constructing a calendar on screen for the month of January 1984. With the FORMAT WIDTH command, format columns 2 through 8 to a width of 8 characters. Move the cell pointer to R2C1, and with the Alpha command, type **January 84**. Move the cell pointer to R2C2; this cell will represent the first day of January, and you're going to use the function COLUMN to enter a 1 at this location. To do this, press Value and then type **COLUMN ()** and **−1** (to subtract 1 from column number 2). The command line shows

VALUE: COLUMN()−1

Press ENTER and the value 1 appears in R2C2. Now use the Copy command to copy this function to the next six columns. The screen now appears as follows:

```
#1        1        2        3        4        5        6        7        8        9
   1
   2 JANUARY 84        1        2        3        4        5        6        7
   3
   4
```

Move the cell pointer to R6C2 to begin the second week. This first cell will represent day 8. The cell pointer is in column 2; to find a value of 8, type the formula **COLUMN()+6**. Press ENTER and an 8 appears in R6C2. Again use the Copy command to copy the formula to the next six columns. To enter the third week, move the cell pointer to R10C2 and type the formula **COLUMN()+13**; again, copy this formula to the next six columns. For the fourth week, move the cell pointer to R14C2; enter and copy the formula COLUMN()+20. To enter the final days of January, use the COLUMN function to obtain day 29 in cell R18C2 and then copy the formula for the next two columns, January 30 and 31. When the January calendar is complete, it looks like Figure 11-1.

Clear the screen with the TRANSFER CLEAR command.

#1	1	2	3	4	5	6	7	8	9
1									
2	JANUARY 84	1	2	3	4	5	6	7	
3									
4									
5									
6		8	9	10	11	12	13	14	
7									
8									
9									
10		15	16	17	18	19	20	21	
11									
12									
13									
14		22	23	24	25	26	27	28	
15									
16									
17									
18		29	30	31					
19									
20									

Figure 11-1. *Calendar constructed by use of the COLUMN function and the COPY command*

ROW

Use of the ROW function, which returns the row number of the cell pointer location, is similar to use of the COLUMN function. Its format is ROW(). To try it, move the cell pointer to R7C3, press **Value**, and type **ROW()**. Press ENTER and the value 7 is entered in R7C3.

Use the Blank command to erase the value in R7C3, and press the HOME key to move the cell pointer to R1C1.

The ROW and COLUMN functions can make it easier to build certain worksheets, such as the TIMES TABLE you developed in Chapter 4. You'll now see how easily it can be done with these functions.

In preparation, use the FORMAT WIDTH command to format columns 2 through 7 of your display to a width of 6. You'll enter times tables for the range of 1×1 to 6×6. Move the cell pointer to R2C2, and after pressing **Value**, type **(ROW()−1)*(COLUMN()−1)**. The command line displays the following:

VALUE: (ROW()−1)*(COLUMN()−1)

Press ENTER and the number 1 appears in R2C2. As you can see, the row and column numbers are serving as increments for factors in the times table.

Before you copy this formula to complete the table, notice the sets of parentheses surrounding the two functions. As discussed in Chapter 7, these parentheses are necessary to the sequence of operations used in solving the formula. If the functions were not set apart by parentheses, the formula would result in a value of -1. Without parentheses, the formula is evaluated in the following order:

1. $-1*COLUMN() = -2$
2. $ROW()-2 = 0$
3. $0-1 = -1$

Constructing the times table necessitates the outer set of parentheses for each function in the formula so that the calculations produce the desired result. If any formula you enter does not produce the results you expect, check the placement of parentheses.

Now use the Copy command once to copy the formula into the block that will complete the desired table. With the cell pointer in R2C2, press Copy and From. The "cells:" field displays R2C2, the correct value. Press the TAB key to move to the "to cells:" field and enter R2C2:R7C7. The command line displays the following:

COPY FROM cells:R2C2   to cells:R2C2:R7C7

Press ENTER, and with the entry of just one formula and one Copy command, you have a complete times table:

#1	1	2	3	4	5	6	7	8	9	10
1										
2		1	2	3	4	5	6			
3		2	4	6	8	10	12			
4		3	6	9	12	15	18			
5		4	8	12	16	20	24			
6		5	10	15	20	25	30			
7		6	12	18	24	30	36			

The DOLLAR, FIXED, and VALUE Functions

When working with functions, you should be aware of whether the value returned is numeric or text. It is not always obvious from the name of the function; for example, the DOLLAR and FIXED functions return text values. If you wish to perform mathematical operations on these values, you can convert them to numeric values by using the VALUE function.

DOLLAR

The DOLLAR function returns its argument as a text value formatted with a dollar sign to the left and two decimal places. If the argument is negative, the text value will be displayed in parentheses (the standard accounting practice) instead of with a minus sign. The format for this function is DOLLAR(N), where N stands for any number.

To prepare for trying this function, use the TRANSFER CLEAR command to put all worksheet values in the default format. Place the cell pointer in column 1, and with the FORMAT cells command, format column 1 to display three decimal places. Format column 2 to right-justify the data entered.

Starting in the home position, press **Value** and then type the following numbers in column 1:

1236.432
43.87
−21.456
0.56
−173.438

Move the cell pointer to R1C2 and enter the following formula:

VALUE: DOLLAR(RC[−1])

Press ENTER and R1C2 displays $1236.43. This is the text value returned by the DOLLAR function with argument 1236.432. Copy the formula to display the DOLLAR function format of the remaining numbers. Your screen display should look like this:

```
#1        1          2          3        4        5        6        7
 1    1236.432    $1236.43
 2      43.870      $43.87
 3     -21.456     ($21.46)
 4       0.560       $0.56
 5    -173.438    ($173.44)
```

Notice the parentheses used to signify negative numbers.

If you SUM the values currently displayed in column 2, the result will be zero—because DOLLAR returns a text value, and a text value has a numeric value of 0. If you need to display dollars and cents *and* perform calculations on those values, you can use the dollar format in the FORMAT cells command or use the VALUE function to change the text values to numeric values.

FIXED

The FIXED function returns a number as a text value displayed with a specified number of decimal places. The format is FIXED(N,Digits) where the argument N can be any number and the argument Digits is a number that tells Multiplan how many digits to print after the decimal point.

You'll use the same set of data to illustrate the FIXED function, so don't clear your screen. Move the cell pointer to R1C3 and format column 3 so the data entered will be right-justified. Now, after pressing **Value**, enter the formula shown on the following command line:

VALUE: FIXED(RC[−2],1)

(The relative reference RC[−2] represents the number 1236.432, and 1 is the number of digits to place after the decimal point.)

Copy the formula down column 3 to display the values in column 1 as specified in the formula. Your screen should look like this:

#1	1	2	3	4	5	6	7
1	1236.432	$1236.43	1236.4				
2	43.870	$43.87	43.9				
3	−21.456	($21.46)	−21.5				
4	0.560	$0.56	0.6				
5	−173.438	($173.44)	−173.4				

What do you think would happen if you tried to use the SUM function to find the sum of the values in column 3? Try it to see if your prediction is correct.

VALUE

The most commonly used command in Multiplan is Value. Multiplan also has a *function* with the name VALUE. The two functions you just worked with, DOLLAR and FIXED, turned numeric values into text data. The purpose of the VALUE function in Multiplan is to turn numbers that are represented as text into numeric values. The format for the VALUE function is VALUE(T), where the argument T stands for text.

You'll use the VALUE command now to change the text in column 3 back to numeric data. Move the cell pointer to R1C4 and, after pressing **Value**, enter the following formula:

VALUE: VALUE(RC[−1])

Press ENTER and R1C4 displays the value 1236.4. The value in R1C4 looks just the same as the one in R1C3, but there is one difference: Column 3 contains text data and column 4 contains numeric data. (Because the entry in column 4 is numeric, it is displayed with one space to the right of the last digit, as are all numeric entries.) Copy the formula from R1C4 down to the next four rows, and your screen looks like this:

#1	1	2	3	4	5	6	7
1	1236.432	$1236.43	1236.4	1236.4			
2	43.870	$43.87	43.9	43.9			
3	-21.456	($21.46)	-21.5	-21.5			
4	0.560	$0.56	0.6	0.6			
5	-173.438	($173.44)	-173.4	-173.4			

To further compare the DOLLAR function to the FORMAT cells command $ format code, use the VALUE function to display the numeric values that are the equivalents of the text values in column 3. To do this, place your cell pointer in R1C5, press Value, and enter this formula:

VALUE: VALUE(RC[−3])

Copy the formula down to the next four rows. The values in column 5 are the same as the text in column 2, but the display is slightly different because the dollar signs are no longer shown and negative numbers are indicated by minus signs instead of parentheses.

Now use the FORMAT cells command to format column 5, rows 1 through 5, with the $ format code. When you have done this, the command lines show

FORMAT cells: R1C5:R5C5   alignment:Def Ctr Gen Left Right-
format code: Def Cont Exp Fix Gen Int ($) * % − # of decimals:

When column 5 is reformatted, the screen looks like this:

#1	1	2	3	4	5	6	7
1	1236.432	$1236.43	1236.4	1236.4	$1236.43		
2	43.870	$43.87	43.9	43.9	$43.87		
3	-21.456	($21.46)	-21.5	-21.5	($21.46)		
4	0.560	$0.56	0.6	0.6	$0.56		
5	-173.438	($173.44)	-173.4	-173.4	($173.44)		

Notice that columns 2 and 5 now look exactly the same except that in column 5 the decimal points are lined up. If you used the SUM function to total the values in column 5, it would return the value $1085.96. If you want to align a column of dollar values, or if you wish to perform arithmetic calculations on dollar values, the $ format code in the FORMAT cells command is a better choice than the DOLLAR function.

The ROUND Function

The ROUND function is used to round numbers and display them to a specified level of precision. Unlike the FIXED function, which returns text values, the ROUND function returns numeric values.

The format for the ROUND function is ROUND(N,Digits), where N is any number and the Digits argument specifies the level of precision. The number in the Digits argument can be positive, zero, or negative. If the number is positive, the value returned will display that many digits after the decimal. If the number is zero, the number value returned will be rounded to the nearest whole number. If the number is negative, the function returns the number rounded to that power of ten (for example, -1 returns values to the nearest multiple of 10, -2 to the nearest multiple of 100, and so on).

Now try some examples. Use the TRANSFER CLEAR command to return your worksheet to default values; then type the following numbers in column 1, rows 1 through 5:

901
23.8765
654.9
1994
0.9876

You can now enter formulas.

1. In R1C2 enter **ROUND(RC[−1],3)**.
2. In R1C3 enter **ROUND(RC[−2],0)**.
3. In R1C4 enter **ROUND(RC[−3],−1)**.
4. In R1C5 enter **ROUND(RC[−3],−3)**.

Copy each of the formulas down through row 5 and your screen displays

#1	1	2	3	4	5	6	7
1	901	901	901	900	1000		
2	23.8765	23.877	24	20	0		
3	654.9	654.9	655	650	1000		
4	1994	1994	1994	1990	2000		
5	0.9876	0.988	1	0	0		

As you can see, the format of the numbers displayed is not consistent, but the values are rounded to be as precise as possible within the constraints of the Digits argument.

The MAX, MIN, and STDEV Functions

The three functions MAX, MIN, and STDEV return the maximum value, minimum value, and standard deviation from an argument containing a list of numbers. The formats for the three functions are

MAX(List)
MIN(List)
STDEV(List)

These functions can be used to compare student test scores or any other type of statistical data, such as sales or expense figures. For an example here, let's use test data. To begin, use the TRANSFER CLEAR command to clear the screen. Then format the worksheet as follows:

```
#1       1          2        3         4         5        6        7
  1     SCORES                MAXIMUM  SCORE =              263
  2   ==========             MINIMUM  SCORE =              199
  3       234                STANDARD DEVIATION =21.660255
  4       251
  5       263
  6       208
  7       199
  8       255
  9       210
 10       229
 11       218
 12       238
```

Figure 11-2.   *Scores entered by use of MAX, MIN and STDEV functions*

1. Right-justify the data for cell R1C1 and type the title **SCORES**.
2. Use the Name command to have the title SCORES refer to cells R3C1:R12C1.
3. Move the cell pointer to R2C1 and type separators (=) across the column.
4. Move the cell pointer to R1C3 and format the block R1C3:R3C4 as continuous.

You are now ready to enter data.

5. In column 1, rows 3 through 12, type the following ten test scores: **234, 251, 263, 208, 199, 255, 210, 229, 218,** and **238**.
6. In R1C3 type the text **MAXIMUM SCORE =**.
7. In R2C3 type the text **MINIMUM SCORE =**.
8. In R3C3 type the text **STANDARD DEVIATION =**.

Now you can enter formulas.

9. In R1C5 type **MAX(SCORES)**.
10. In R2C5 type **MIN(SCORES)**.
11. In R3C5 type **STDEV(SCORES)**.

The functions should cause the values shown in Figure 11-2 to be displayed.

Using Functions as Arguments

You can combine functions in formulas as you did earlier in this chapter when you built the times table. You can also combine functions in formulas by using one function as an argument for another. In fact, some functions are used almost exclusively as arguments for other functions. Now you'll try using a function as an argument by combining the FIXED function with the STDEV function.

The standard deviation of test scores calculated in the previous section of this chapter is displayed to six decimal places. There is no need for so many, so you can use the FIXED function to control the number of decimal places displayed. In fact, you can use a single formula to calculate the standard deviation *and* control the decimal places displayed:

FIXED(STDEV(SCORES),2)

Now edit the entry in cell R3C5 so it includes the function FIXED (STDEV(SCORES),2). This formula parallels the format for the FIXED function, FIXED(N,Digits): STDEV(SCORES) returns a number that becomes the N argument for the FIXED function, and you enter the number 2 for the Digits argument. Press ENTER and the value returned to R3C5 is 21.66, which represents the standard deviation displayed to two decimal places. The entry is left-justified because you have not changed from the default format and because the FIXED function returns a text value.

Before considering the next functions, use the TRANSFER CLEAR command to clear the screen and return the worksheet to the default format.

The LEN, MID, and INT Functions

The LEN and MID functions are used with text data and many times are used in the same formula. The INT function is quite versatile and can be used with many functions, as you will soon see when you use it with the MID function.

LEN

The function LEN is used to find the length of a text value. The format is LEN(T), where T stands for the text value. As pointed out earlier, some functions, in practical use, are used almost exclusively as arguments for other functions. This is true of the LEN function, but first you'll try it in its simplest format.

To illustrate the LEN function, format R1C1:2 to be continuous and type the name **SMITH, FRANK A.** in R1C1. Then move the cell pointer to R2C1. The length of the text value in R1C1 may be determined by pressing **Value** and entering either of the following formulas:

VALUE:LEN(R1C1)
VALUE:LEN(R[−1]C)

In either case, when you press ENTER, the number 15 is returned to R2C1. This number represents the length of the text in R1C1, including punctuation marks and spaces.

The text for the LEN argument can be entered directly into the formula

LEN("SMITH, FRANK A.")

When you enter text for a text argument directly into a formula, you must enclose the text in double quotation marks as shown. As you might expect, you can also use the Name command to reference a cell in a function argument. If NAME refers to R1C1, LEN(NAME) will return a value of 15.

MID

The MID function is one of those functions most commonly used in conjunction with other functions. First you'll use the function in a simple format so that you can get used to entering its arguments, and then you'll use it with INT to graph data.

The MID function returns a portion of a text value. The format is MID(T,Start,Count), where T represents the text value, Start is the position at which the text returned should begin, and Count is the number of characters you wish returned from the starting position.

For example, assume you wish to display the first name of SMITH, FRANK A. from cell R1C1. The name FRANK starts at the eighth character and extends for five characters. Move the cell pointer to R3C1. You can display the name FRANK by entering any one of the following three formulas:

MID(R[−2]C,8,5)
MID(R1C1,8,5)
MID("SMITH, FRANK A.", 8,5)

When you press ENTER, the text value FRANK is returned. You can also designate the text value in the MID argument by using Name reference.

INT

The integer function, INT, eliminates the decimal portion of any number displayed as a decimal. The format for the INT function is INT(N), where N is the number reduced to the next *smallest* whole number. For example:

INT(7.3) returns 7
INT(5.98) returns 5

When the INT function is used, the value returned is not rounded, but instead represents the next smallest whole number. When the N argument is a negative number, the whole-number portion of the decimal will be incremented down one whole number. For example:

INT(−12.99) returns −13
INT(−12.01) returns −13

Try these and a few more examples of your own choosing to be sure you understand how the INT function works.

The INT and MID functions can be used together to assign letter grades to a set of student scores that are shown in percents. To do this, begin by using the TRANSFER CLEAR command to clear the screen.

Move the cell pointer to R1C1 and type **PERCENT**; then move to R1C2 and type **GRADE**. With the FORMAT cells command, right-justify the data in R1C1:2. Type the = as a separator in R2C1:2; and in column 1, starting in row 3, type the following percents: **93.3**, **48.8**, **73.6**, **78.1**, **81.8**, and **98.0**. Using the FORMAT cells command, display the data in column 1 with one decimal point. Your worksheet should look like this:

```
#1        1          2        3       4       5       6       7
 1      PERCENT     GRADE
 2    ====================
 3       93.3
 4       48.8
 5       73.6
 6       78.1
 7       81.8
 8       98.0
```

Move the cell pointer to R3C2, press Value, and enter the formula so your command line matches the following:

VALUE: MID("FFFFFDCBAA",INT(RC[−1]/10),1)

Before you press ENTER, consider the arguments for the MID function. Enclosed in double quotation marks is the text value that contains the letter grades. As you will see soon, this string of grades is entered in sequence according to test score percents: 10–59% earns an F grade; 60–69% earns a D, 70–79% earns a C, 80–89% earns a B, and 90–100% earns an A. (Note: If the percent grade is less than 10, the formula will return an error message. After reading Chapter 12, which deals with logical values, you will have the tools to adjust the formula to avoid that error — or you can just drop the student.)

The second argument, Start, determines where you will begin in the text value; it takes the INT of the percent divided by 10, which will always give a single digit in the range 1–10. The final argument, Count, has the value 1, which means you want only one character returned from the text value.

The test score percent in R3C1 is 93.3. When this number is divided by 10, the result is 9.33. Using the INT function returns a value of 9. The MID function, then, returns one character of the text value starting at the ninth position, which is to say it returns an A. Press ENTER and an A grade will be assigned in R3C2. Copy the MID and INT formulas down the next five rows, and the appropriate letter grade is assigned to each percent as follows:

```
#1        1         2        3       4        5        6        7
  1     PERCENT    GRADE
  2   =====================
  3      93.3        A
  4      48.8        F
  5      73.6        C
  6      78.1        C
  7      81.8        B
  8      98.0        A
```

The LOOKUP Function

The LOOKUP function is one of the most powerful functions found in any computer spreadsheet program. For instance, Lookup tables are useful in worksheets that use price lists or discount schedules. LOOKUP allows you to extract one item from a table or block of data associated with a numerical argument. The format for the function is LOOKUP(N,Table), where N stands for a number and Table represents a block of data.

To see how the LOOKUP function is used, you'll develop a worksheet to calculate payroll tax withholding. To begin, format a worksheet and enter data to match the screen shown in Figure 11-3. Use the Name command to assign the employee names to their salaries (for example, assign the name BREWSTER to cell R4C2).

The worksheet is divided into two parts. The top portion lists three employees and their salaries, along with the number of dependents for each. The two blank columns in this top portion, labeled TAX and TAX*, will contain each employee's tax determined by the LOOKUP function. It is divided into two columns so that you can determine an intermediate tax in the column labeled TAX and the exact tax in the column labeled TAX*. The bottom portion of Figure 11-3, rows 11 through 15 and columns 1 through 5, contains all the data to be used by the LOOKUP function; this *Lookup table* consists of a tax table with salary ranges in column 1 and the tax on each salary according to the number of

#1	1	2	3	4	5	6	7
1							
2							
3		SALARY	DEP.	TAX	TAX*		
4	BREWSTER	457	1				
5	CUNNINGHAM	523	2				
6	WALTERS	397	0				
7							
8							
9	TAX TABLE (MARRIED)						
10		(0)	(1)	(2)			
11	350	25	19	13	0.05		
12	400	30	14	18	0.07		
13	450	35	29	23	0.09		
14	500	40	34	28	0.10		
15	550	45	39	33	0.11		
16							
17							
18							

Figure 11-3.   *Worksheet for use of the LOOKUP function*

dependents. The number in column 5 shows the percentage (converted to a decimal) that will be multiplied by the employee's wages over the base amount of column 1.

Consider the first employee, Brewster. Because his salary is $457, it falls in the tax range between $450 and $500. This employee has one dependent, so looking in the table, you can see his base tax is $29. You can also determine that the base tax for Cunningham is $28 and for Walters is $25. However, your purpose here is not to look this up in the tables, but rather to have Multiplan determine it for you.

Now look at Figure 11-4. Since Brewster has one dependent, you don't need to assign all the data in the tax table to the Lookup table. Only the portion indicated in the figure is required. LOOKUP(N,R11C1:R15C3) assigns this section of the tax data to the LOOKUP function. For the other two employees, the portions of the tax data to be used in the Lookup table will change since they each have a different number of dependents. The data in column 5 of the TAX TABLE will be included in the Lookup table in the final portion of this chapter when you find the exact tax for each employee.

Now let's have Multiplan determine Brewster's tax. Move the cell pointer to R4C4; press **Value** and enter the following formula:

LOOKUP(BREWSTER,R11C1:R15C3)

The name BREWSTER designates the employee's salary, 457, and the cell range

#1	1	2	3	4	5	6	7
1							
2							
3		SALARY	DEP.	TAX	TAX*		
4	BREWSTER	457	1				
5	CUNNINGHAM	523	2				
6	WALTERS	397	0				
7							
8							
9	TAX TABLE (MARRIED)						
10		(0)	(1)	(2)			
11	350	25	19	13	0.05		
12	400	30	14	18	0.07		
13	450	35	29	23	0.09		
14	500	40	34	28	0.10		
15	550	45	39	33	0.11		
16							
17							
18							

Figure 11-4.   *LOOKUP table for Brewster is framed here*

R11C1:R15C3 refers to the table that includes the salaries and tax amounts for one dependent. Multiplan looks in the first column of the table and finds the highest value in column 1 that is less than Brewster's salary—in this case, 450—and then extracts the data from the last column of that same row in the table, which is 29—remember, you have selected only up to column 3 for Brewster—and returns 29 to cell R4C4, which contains the formula. Press ENTER and 29 is printed in R4C4.

Now move the cell pointer to R5C4 and enter the appropriate formula for Cunningham. Press Value and type **LOOKUP**. Then press F3 and the right arrow key until the name CUNNINGHAM appears. Type a , and enter the appropriate range for the table, R11C1:R15C4. Notice that this time you include column 4 because Cunningham has two dependents and Multiplan will extract the data from the last column in the table. Press ENTER and 28 appears in R5C4.

Use the same procedure to enter the appropriate formula for Walters. The correct formula is

LOOKUP(WALTERS,R11C1:R15C2)

Again the table boundaries change because Walters has zero dependents. Press ENTER and 25 appears in R6C4. Your worksheet now looks like Figure 11-5.

If Brewster earned $450, his tax in column 3, $29, would be correct. But he earns $7 more, so you have to use the percent in the last column of the TAX

#1	1	2	3	4	5	6	7
1							
2							
3		SALARY	DEP.	TAX	TAX*		
4	BREWSTER	457	1	29			
5	CUNNINGHAM	523	2	28			
6	WALTERS	397	0	25			
7							
8							
9	TAX TABLE (MARRIED)						
10		(0)	(1)	(2)			
11	350	25	19	13	0.05		
12	400	30	14	18	0.07		
13	450	35	29	23	0.09		
14	500	40	34	28	0.10		
15	550	45	39	33	0.11		
16							
17							
18							

Figure 11-5.   *Tax entries made by use of LOOKUP function*

TABLE and apply that to the amount he earned over $450. The calculation for Brewster's actual tax is:

$$29 + (457-450) \times 9\%$$
$$= 29 + 7 \times 0.09$$
$$= 29.63$$

Now you can build the formula that Multiplan will use to determine this tax. You have already found 29 with the formula

LOOKUP(BREWSTER,R11C1:R15C3)

You can enter the next portion of the formula, 457–450, as:

BREWSTER–LOOKUP(BREWSTER,R11C1:R15C1)

You find the final part of the formula, the percentage multiplier, by entering:

LOOKUP(BREWSTER,R11C1:R15C5)

With the cell pointer in R4C5, combine these calculations into one formula and enter it as follows:

```
#1       1            2            3          4          5          6          7
  1
  2
  3                 SALARY       DEP.        TAX        TAX*
  4 BREWSTER         457          1          29        29.63
  5 CUNNINGHAM       523          2          28        30.30
  6 WALTERS          397          0          25        27.35
  7
  8
  9 TAX TABLE  (MARRIED)
 10                 (0)         (1)        (2)
 11       350        25          19         13        0.05
 12       400        30          14         18        0.07
 13       450        35          29         23        0.09
 14       500        40          34         28        0.10
 15       550        45          39         33        0.11
 16
 17
 18
```

Figure 11-6.   *TAX* entries made by use of LOOKUP function*

VALUE: LOOKUP(BREWSTER,R11C1:R15C3)+(BREWSTER−
LOOKUP(BREWSTER,R11C1:R15C1))∗LOOKUP(BREWSTER,
R11C1:R15C5)

The easiest way to enter the formulas for Cunningham and Walters is to copy
this formula down two rows and then use the Edit command to make the
necessary changes to the table references. Do this now and your screen should
calculate taxes as shown in Figure 11-6.

In this example, the Lookup table was either square or contained more rows
than columns. As you have seen, this caused Multiplan to search for a value in
the first column and return a value from the last column of the same row. If the
Lookup table contained more columns than rows, it would search for a value in
the first row and return a value from the last row of the same column.

Exercises

1. a. Expand the times table developed in this chapter to include the numbers 12×12.
   b. Relocate the beginning of the table so that 1×1 occurs in cell R3C4.
2. Type the following data in column 1, rows 2 through 5: **1327, 986, 1150, 1297, 1301**. Use the MAX, MIN, and STDEV functions to find these values.
3. Use the DOLLAR function to express the data from exercise 2 in $ format with commas where appropriate. Use the necessary functions to find the sum of this data.
4. Enter the following dates in column 1: **03/10/84, 03/16/84, 01/17/84, 02/29/84**, and **03/05/84**. Use the MID function to print only the month in column 2.
5. To the worksheet dealing with LOOKUP add the following data for name, salary, and number of dependents: **Wilson, 433, 2**. Enter the appropriate formulas to determine his base tax and total tax.

Working With
Logical Functions

12

- The AND, OR, and NOT Functions
- The IF-THEN Function
- Coding Data for Regrouping

Functions

- AND
- OR
- NOT
- IF-THEN

Multiplan's logical functions are AND, OR, and NOT. These logical functions are used extensively with the IF-THEN function. Logical functions use *relational operators* to compare two values and then return a value based on that comparison. If you have little or no background in working with logical operators, you may find it useful to study a math or programming text that fully explains their use.

Relational operators are constructed of the equals, less-than, and greater-than signs alone or in various combinations. Table 12-1 lists all the relational operators and gives a simple example of each in use.

You'll use the following worksheet to learn the use of logical functions.

```
#1          1          2          3          4          5          6          7
 1
 2
 3 NAME                 AGE    INCOME     CITY       ZIP
 4 =========================================================================
 5 BABER               53      2100                  94520
 6 FOX                 43      1450                  94522
 7 GOMES               47      1640                  94522
 8 SHORT               50      1400                  94553
 9 WILSON              51      1550                  94520
10
```

Symbol	Meaning	Example
=	equal to	6 = 6
<	less than	4 < 6
>	greater than	7 > 3
<=	less than or equal to	5<=7,5<=5
>=	greater than or equal to	9>=8,8>=8
<>	not equal to	4<>7

Table 12-1.   *Relational Operators Used in Logical Functions*

Enter the worksheet and data now:

1. Right-justify the titles, AGE to ZIP in row 3.
2. Format row 4 continuous in columns 1 through 7.
3. Use the REPT function to generate the separator in row 4.
4. Format the data in the block R3C2:R9C5 to be right-justified.
5. Assign the following names to data:

   AGE to R5:9C2
   INCOME to R5:9C3
   ZIP to R5:9C5

You're ready to learn about logical functions in Multiplan.

The AND, OR, and NOT Functions

The logical functions AND, OR, and NOT return values of TRUE and FALSE. They are used to compare values in a list, and if the conditions of the function are met, a value of TRUE is returned. If the conditions of the function are *not* met, a value of FALSE is returned.

AND

The AND function compares a list of relational statements in its argument. If all of the statements in the list are true, the AND function returns TRUE; if one (or more) of the statements is not true, the AND function returns FALSE. The format for the AND function is AND(List), where List represents a list of relational statements.

You're going to use the AND function to print TRUE if a person is over the age of 50 and has an income greater than $1500. If either condition is false, the function returns FALSE. The formula to perform this function is

AND(AGE>50,INCOME>1500)

What this formula says is, *if* AGE is greater than 50 *AND* INCOME is greater than 1500, then TRUE.

Move the cell pointer to R5C6; using the Value command, type the formula just shown. Press ENTER and you'll see the value TRUE displayed. Use the Copy command to copy the formula down the next four rows:

```
#1          1           2           3           4           5           6           7
 1
 2
 3 NAME                AGE         INCOME      CITY        ZIP
 4 ========================================================================
 5 BABER               53          2100                    94520        TRUE
 6 FOX                 43          1450                    94522        FALSE
 7 GOMES               47          1640                    94522        FALSE
 8 SHORT               50          1400                    94553        FALSE
 9 WILSON              51          1550                    94520        TRUE
10
```

OR

The OR function returns TRUE if *any* of the relational statements in the List is true. The format is OR(List).

Now identify the people who are either over age 50 or have an income greater than $1500, or both. Move the cell pointer to R5C7 and type the following formula:

OR(AGE>50,INCOME>1500)

Press ENTER. A value of TRUE is returned. Copy the formula down to the next four rows. Can you predict the results before you press ENTER? Press ENTER and your screen displays

```
#1          1           2           3           4           5           6           7
 1
 2
 3 NAME                AGE         INCOME      CITY        ZIP
 4 ========================================================================
 5 BABER               53          2100                    94520        TRUE        TRUE
 6 FOX                 43          1450                    94522        FALSE       FALSE
 7 GOMES               47          1640                    94522        FALSE       TRUE
 8 SHORT               50          1400                    94553        FALSE       FALSE
 9 WILSON              51          1550                    94520        TRUE        TRUE
10
```

NOT

The NOT function can be used to give the opposite result of the AND and OR functions; it changes a TRUE value to FALSE and a FALSE value to TRUE. The format is NOT(Logical), where Logical is a logical function.

You can use the NOT function in conjunction with the AND function to determine the people who are *not* over age 50 *and do not* have an income greater than $1500. You'll edit the AND function in column 6 to do this.

Move the cell pointer back to R5C6 and press **Edit**. Move the edit cursor to the beginning of the formula and type **NOT**, and then enclose the remaining formula in parentheses. The command line should display

EDIT: NOT(AND(AGE>50,INCOME>$1500))

Press ENTER and the value returned is FALSE. Copy the formula down four rows and those values will also change.

The IF-THEN Function

The IF-THEN function is used to return a value based on the TRUE or FALSE result of a Logical argument. If the Logical argument returns a value of TRUE, the IF-THEN function returns a specified value; if the Logical argument returns a value of FALSE, the IF-THEN function returns a different specified value. The format for the IF-THEN function is IF(Logical,Then Value,Else Value), where the Then Value represents the value returned if the Logical argument is TRUE, and the Else Value represents the value returned if the Logical argument is FALSE.

We can use the IF-THEN function to assign city names according to the ZIP codes in the sample worksheet. Move the cell pointer to R5C4 and type this formula:

IF(ZIP<94530,"CONCORD","MARTINEZ")

According to this formula, if the ZIP code is less than 94530, then return the text value CONCORD; if the ZIP code is not less than 94530, then return the text value MARTINEZ. This formula is correct because the two ZIP codes 94520 and 94522 are in the city of Concord, and ZIP code 94553 is in the city of Martinez.

Press ENTER and the city name CONCORD is assigned to row 5. Copy the formula down to the next four rows and the appropriate city will be entered in column 4. Your worksheet now looks like the following:

```
#1        1          2        3         4          5        6         7
 1
 2
 3  NAME              AGE    INCOME     CITY       ZIP
 4  ===========================================================================
 5  BABER             53     2100     CONCORD     94520    FALSE     TRUE
 6  FOX               43     1450     CONCORD     94522    TRUE      FALSE
 7  GOMES             47     1640     CONCORD     94522    TRUE      TRUE
 8  SHORT             50     1400     MARTINEZ    94553    TRUE      FALSE
 9  WILSON            51     1550     CONCORD     94520    FALSE     TRUE
10
```

The Then Value and Else Value arguments can return either text values or numeric values. Which type of values is returned can be determined by any one of several ways: by direct entry in the formula; by using Name, absolute, and relative references; or by performing calculations on data. For example, return just the city name CONCORD to column 6 of the current worksheet. Blank the section R5:9C6:7, move the cell pointer to R5C6, and enter the following formula:

IF(ZIP<94530,RC[−2]," ")

When you press ENTER, CONCORD will appear in R5C6. Here you used relative referencing to print the text value, but you could have used either absolute or Name referencing. Note also that two double quotation marks are used to return a blank space for the Else Value, and that the Then Value and Else Value are always separated by a comma.

Coding Data for Regrouping

As mentioned in Chapter 8, data like expense items can be separated, regrouped, and rearranged by codes. You can develop a simple worksheet that illustrates this function.

Clear the current worksheet and enter the data shown in the following worksheet:

#1	1	2	3	4	5	6	7
1	1	23					
2	1	65					
3	2	23					
4	1	12					
5	2	90					
6	3	54					
7	2	56					
8	1	11					
9							
10							

First you'll use the IF function to print the numbers from column 2 that have a code of 1 in column 1. Move the cell pointer to R1C3 and enter the following formula:

IF(RC[−2]=1,RC[−1],0)

The formula tells Multiplan that if the value in column 1 is 1, then print the value from column 2 in column 3; if the value in column 1 is not 1, then print a 0 in column 3.

Press ENTER and the value 23 is printed in R1C3. Use the Copy command to copy the formula down seven rows. All the numbers from column 2 that have a code of 1 are displayed in column 3, and all other numbers are represented by a 0. You can now use the SUM function to sum the values in column 3, or you can perform any other operation you desire.

Now let's print values in column 4 that have a code in column 1 of either 1 or 2. Enter the formula displayed on the following command line:

VALUE: IF(OR(RC[−3]=1,RC[−3]=2),RC[−2],0)

The formula says that if the value in column 1 is either 1 or 2, then print the value from column 2 in column 4; otherwise, print a 0. Press ENTER and 23 is printed in R1C4. Copy the formula down seven rows. The worksheet now looks like this:

#1	1	2	3	4	5	6	7
1	1	23	23	23			
2	1	65	65	65			
3	2	23	0	23			
4	1	12	12	12			
5	2	90	0	90			
6	3	54	0	0			
7	2	56	0	56			
8	1	11	11	11			
9							

The logical functions AND, OR, and NOT and the IF-THEN function allow much data manipulation with the Multiplan worksheet. The next chapter presents some more advanced examples of their use.

Exercises

1. Using the following data, write a logical expression to print TRUE or FALSE in column 6 for people who are less than 50, have an income greater than $1500, and live in Concord.

```
#1      1       2       3       4       5       6       7
 1
 2
 3 NAME         AGE   INCOME    CITY     ZIP
 4 ==========================================================
 5 BABER        53     2100    CONCORD   94520
 6 FOX          43     1450    CONCORD   94522
 7 GOMES        47     1640    CONCORD   94522
 8 SHORT        50     1400    MARTINEZ  94553
 9 WILSON       51     1550    CONCORD   94520
10
```

2. Using the data from Exercise 1, write a logical expression to print TRUE in column 7 for people who are over 50 or who have income greater than $1500.

3. Using the January budget worksheet from Chapter 10, build a formula with appropriate functions to print the amounts in column 8 of those items having a code of 2 or 3.

4. Using the TEST SCORES worksheet in Chapter 9, print each student's letter grade in column 8. Again use the logical functions developed in this chapter to build the formulas.

5. Again using the TEST SCORES worksheet and the logical functions, write a formula that will print PASS for each student with a percent score greater than or equal to 60, and FAIL if the score is less than 60.

The Iteration
Process

- The ITERCNT Function
- The ISNA Function
- The TRUE and FALSE Functions
- Iteration: A Step at a Time
- The INDEX Function
- Subtotaling Coded Lists
- The ISERROR Function
- The NA Function
- The DELTA Function
- The NPV Function

Functions

- ITERCNT
- ISNA
- TRUE
- FALSE
- INDEX

- ISERROR
- NA
- DELTA
- NPV

Iterate, like *reiterate,* means to repeat again and again. In this chapter you'll apply this concept to mathematical formulas in which calculations repeat again and again to change the results.

Use the TRANSFER CLEAR command to set all the format options to default values. Move the cell pointer to R1C1 and, using the Value command, type **RC+1**. This formula will add a value of 1 to the current contents of the active cell; initially the value of R1C1 is 0, so the calculation will be 1 + 0. Press ENTER, and a value of 1 is entered in R1C1 and the message line displays, "Unresolved circular references." This message means that if Multiplan calculated the formula in R1C1 a second time, the result would change; with R1C1 now equal to 1, the second calculation would be 1 + 1 and give a value of 2.

In the default format, Multiplan calculates the value for the cell only once, but if a recalculation would change the value of the cell, Multiplan prints the "Unresolved circular references" message. You can cause Multiplan to repeat calculations again and again. This process is called *iteration.*

The idea of "recalc" (recalculate) was introduced in Chapter 10, so be sure that you don't confuse recalculation with iteration. You'll recall that if Multiplan is in its default state (that is, with the "recalc:" field of the Options command line set to Yes), calculations are automatically performed each time data is entered in a cell. If recalc is off ("recalc:" set to No), worksheet calculations are made only when you press F4. Iteration, however, is a special process that repeats calculations again and again until either (1) Multiplan reaches the limits of number reporting, or (2) it reaches a calculation limit that you set.

Iteration is invoked just as recalc is — by use of the Options command. Press **O**ptions and your screen displays

OPTIONS recalc: (Yes) No   Mute: Yes(No)
           iteration: Yes(No)   Completion test at:

Change the response in the "iteration:" field to Yes. If you press ENTER, Multiplan will repeatedly recalculate the value in cell R1C1, each time adding a value of 1 to the current value so the number is continually increased by 1. This iteration process can be stopped by pressing the ESC key.

Press ENTER now. The value in R1C1 changes very rapidly. Press ESC and the iteration stops. The value in the cell will depend on how long you allowed the iteration process to continue.

To control the iteration process you can specify a "completion test" to be used with the iteration process. The final Options command field, "completion test at:", allows you to place in a cell a condition that will cause the iteration process to stop.

Clear your screen and move the cell pointer to R5C1. You'll place a condition here that causes iteration to stop when the value in R1C1 reaches 20. With the Value command enter this formula:

VALUE: R[−4]C=20

Press ENTER. Since the content of R1C1 is 0, Multiplan returns FALSE in R5C1. Press **O**ptions and enter the responses to each field so that your command line matches the following display:

OPTIONS recalc: (Yes)No   Mute: Yes(No)
           iteration: (Yes)No   Completion test at: R5C1

Press ENTER and move the cell pointer to the home position. Enter the formula RC+1 again. Press ENTER and the value in R1C1 increases until it reaches 20. Then the iteration process stops, and the value in R5C1 is changed to TRUE.

There are several functions that are used with the iteration option, and they are the subject of the remainder of this chapter.

The ITERCNT Function

ITERCNT stands for "ITERation CouNT." This function returns the number of times that Multiplan has recalculated a formula. The format is ITERCNT(). There are no arguments in the function, but parentheses are still required.

Clear the screen using the TRANSFER CLEAR command. (Note: If your version of Multiplan is not IBM version 1.1 for PC DOS, the TRANSFER CLEAR command may not set the "iteration:" field of the Options command to No. If this is true for your version, each time you are instructed to use the TRANSFER CLEAR command in this chapter, also enter the Options command and set the "iteration:" field to No.)

You'll now add the ITERCNT() function to the previous example. Move the cell pointer to R1C2, and with the Value command type **ITERCNT( )**. Press ENTER and #N/A is displayed in R1C2. This is the error notation for "number not available." In other words, the iteration count has not yet started.

Move the cell pointer back to R1C1 and type the formula **RC+1**. Press ENTER. Again in R5C1 type **R[−4]C=20**. Select the Options command. In the "iteration:" field, change the response to Yes, and in the "completion test at:" field, enter R5C1. Press ENTER. The value in R1C1 rapidly changes until it reaches 20. The value in R5C1 changes to TRUE, and the iteration count displayed in R1C2 is 18. The value 18 is two counts behind the value in R1C1 because the first time through there is no count (it is not available) and then the count starts at the *beginning* of each iteration. The count was stopped during the nineteenth iteration, when the value in R1C1 changed from 19 to 20, and so the final count is 19 − 1, or 18.

The ISNA Function

The ISNA function returns the logical value TRUE if the value you asked for is not available. ISNA stands for "IS Not Available." The format is ISNA(Value).

This function will be included in the next example, in which you will use the iteration process to find the cube root of a number. (Your purpose here is only to see another characteristic of iteration; you'll learn a better method of finding the cube root of a number in Chapter 14.) A cube root is the number that, when multiplied by itself three times, has a product equal to a specified number. For example, the cube root of 8 is 2, since $2 \times 2 \times 2 = 8$. Use 88 as the number for which you'll find the cube root.

Begin by using the TRANSFER CLEAR command to set all of your format values to default. Now you should do a little planning. The product of $4 \times 4 \times 4$ is 64 and of $5 \times 5 \times 5$ is 125, so the number you are searching for must be a decimal value between 4 and 5. Enter the following formulas in the indicated cells, and see what happens on the screen:

```
R1C1    IF(ISNA(ITERCNT()),4,RC+0.1)
R2C1    R[−1]C*R[−1]C*R[−1]C>88
R3C1    R[−2]C*R[−2]C*R[−2]C
```

Your screen display looks like this:

```
#1          1         2         3         4         5         6         7
  1              4
  2      FALSE
  3             64
  4
  5
```

Press **O**ptions and change the responses in the field to match the following display:

```
OPTIONS recalc:  (Yes)No        Mute:  Yes(No)
         iteration:  (Yes)No     Completion test at:  R2C1
```

Press ENTER and your screen displays

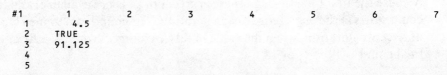

```
#1          1         2         3         4         5         6         7
  1             4.5
  2      TRUE
  3          91.125
  4
  5
```

Now consider what each of the formulas is doing. The formula in R1C1, the first argument for the IF function, is ISNA(ITERCNT()). This is true for the initial iteration since ISNA returns a value of TRUE when the error message #N/A is returned. Since the first argument is true, the second IF argument, 4, is entered in R1C1. On each subsequent iteration, the first argument is false and the value in R1C1 is increased by 0.1 on each pass.

The formula in R2C1 is the completion test. It multiplies the value returned in R1C1 by itself three times and is FALSE until the product is greater than 88. Then the iteration process stops. The value returned in R2C1 will always be either FALSE or TRUE, never a number.

The formula in R3C1 indicates the result of the number in R1C1 multiplied by itself three times, so that you can see how close your value is to the desired result.

The result obtained on this first try (91.125) is not particularly close to the number you're after. You can change the third argument in the IF function to increment in smaller steps, which should yield a more accurate cube root. With the cell pointer in R1C1, press Edit and change the values of the second and third arguments to match the following display:

EDIT: IF(ISNA(ITERCNT()),4.4,RC+0.001)

Press ENTER and the iteration process begins again. On completion you can see that the result in R3C1 is considerably closer to 88.

You can change the third argument of the IF function to get as close to the cube root of 88 as you desire. The accuracy limits of Multiplan is 14 places. The number entered in the second argument, the initial calculation value, will save computer processing time. If you enter a second argument of 4 and an extremely small increment (say 0.00001), you will get a close result the first time; but the result will be a very long time in coming. It is better to change both the initial calculation value and the increment in small steps, rather than use just an extremely small increment.

The TRUE and FALSE Functions

Two other functions available in Multiplan are TRUE and FALSE. Their format is TRUE( ) and FALSE( ). These functions are used mainly to test logical comparisons. In the next section you'll use the TRUE function to move through the iteration process a step at a time.

Iteration: A Step at a Time

Sometimes it's useful to use the iteration process and proceed through a program one step at a time. To try this, use the TRANSFER CLEAR command to clear the screen and enter the following formulas in the cells indicated:

```
R1C1   IF(RC=0,4,RC+0.01)
R2C1   TRUE( )
R3C1   R[-2]C*R[-2]C*R[-2]C
```

Now select the Options command and change the fields to match the following display.

OPTIONS recalc: Yes(No)   Mute: Yes(No)
iteration: (Yes)No   Completion test at: R2C1

Press ENTER. Each time you press the F4 key, the values in R1C1 and R3C1 will change. Because you entered TRUE in R2C1, the cell checked by the completion test, the iteration process stops after each pass.

The INDEX Function

Another function that is useful with the iteration process is INDEX. This function returns the value of a cell located in a specified rectangular area. The format is INDEX(Area,Subscripts). The first argument, Area, represents a set of data. The data may be in a single row or column or in a rectangular block. You can use either one subscript or two. If you use only one, all of the data must be in a single row or column. If the data is in a block, you must use two subscripts.

To see the INDEX function work, use the TRANSFER CLEAR command and then type the following numbers in column 1 beginning at row 2: **23**, **65**, **23**, **12**, **90**, **54**, **56**, **11**. In R1C1 enter the title SCORES and then use the Name command to have it apply to the data. Move the cell pointer to R11C1 and enter the following formula:

INDEX(SCORES,5)

Press ENTER and your screen matches the following display. Notice that the INDEX formula has returned the value of the fifth item in the designated area.

```
#1          1          2          3          4          5          6          7
    1  SCORES
    2          23
    3          65
    4          23
    5          12
    6          90
    7          54
    8          56
    9          11
   10
   11          90
```

Try this once more using a rectangular area. In column 2 enter the following numbers, beginning in row 2: **28**, **70**, **28**, **17**, **95**, **59**, **61**, **16**. Using the Edit command, change the title SCORES to SCORESX. With the Name command apply the name SCORESX in R1C1 to cover the entire block of data R2C1:R9C2. Move the cell pointer down to R13C1 and enter this formula:

INDEX(SCORESX,6,2)

Press ENTER and now your screen displays as follows. The INDEX function returns the value 59, which is the sixth number down in the second column.

#1	1	2	3	4	5	6	7
1	SCORESX						
2	23	28					
3	65	70					
4	23	28					
5	12	17					
6	90	95					
7	54	59					
8	56	61					
9	11	16					
10							
11	90						
12							
13	59						

Subtotaling Coded Lists

You now have the tools necessary to find the sum of a group of numbers in one column that have a specific "code" in another column. Clear your screen and enter the following data:

#1	1	2	3	4	5	6	7
1	CODE	SCORE					
2	1	23					
3	1	65					
4	2	23					
5	1	12					
6	2	90					
7	3	54					
8	2	56					
9	1	11					
10	3	5					
11	3	2					
12	2	45					

You will now sum the numbers in column 2 that have the same code in column 1, this time without moving them to a separate column. To add those numbers with a code of 1, for example, Multiplan must look at each row individually, and if the code in column 1 is 1, add the number in column 2 to the contents of the active cell. If the code is not 1, Multiplan adds a zero to the active cell. To have Multiplan do this, first use the Name command and have the Name reference CODE apply to the data in column 1 and the Name reference SCORE to the data in column 2. Now enter the following formulas in the cells indicated:

```
R13C1  ITERCNT()>=COUNT(CODE)
R13C3  IF(ISNA(ITERCNT()),0,IF(INDEX(CODE,ITERCNT())=1,
         RC+INDEX(SCORE,ITERCNT()),RC))
```

Select the Options command and change the "iteration:" field and "completion test at:" fields to match the following display:

```
OPTIONS    recalc: (Yes)No        Mute: Yes(No)
           iteration: (Yes)No     Completion test at: R13C1
```

Press ENTER and the value in R13C3 changes until the total, 111, appears. The value TRUE appears in R13C1 to indicate that the iteration count is greater than or equal to the number of items in the list, CODE. Your display should look like this:

```
#1         1          2          3      4       5       6       7
  1        CODE       SCORE
  2        1          23
  3        1          65
  4        2          23
  5        1          12
  6        2          90
  7        3          54
  8        2          56
  9        1          11
 10        3           5
 11        3           2
 12        2          45
 13        TRUE                   111
```

The first formula is the completion test formula. It limits the number of iterations to the number of items in the list.

The second formula sums the values with a code of 1. In the first pass the iteration count is not available (#N/A), so ISNA(ITERCNT()) returns TRUE and 0 is placed in R13C3. On the next and each subsequent pass of the iteration process, a portion of the formula, INDEX(CODE,ITERCNT())=1, checks the CODE in column 1.

If the code is equal to 1, Multiplan performs the THEN portion of the formula:

RC+INDEX(SCORE,ITERCNT())

This portion of the formula adds the contents of the active cell, RC, to the value in the SCORE list INDEX(SCORE,ITERCNT()). If the code is not equal to 1, the final portion of the formula, the ELSE portion, is performed:

RC

This portion of the formula means the active cell retains its current value.

The formula is somewhat involved, but if the type of worksheet you use deals with codes, it is worth the time to understand it.

The ISERROR Function

The ISERROR function is similar to the ISNA function. It returns TRUE if *any* of Multiplan's error values are encountered (see Appendix D for a list of error values). By contrast, ISNA returns TRUE only when the Not Available error (#N/A) is found. The format for the ISERROR function is ISERROR(Value).

In the first example in this chapter (the portion of the worksheet with the logical value FALSE returned), ISERROR could replace ISNA without changing the results. Another practical use of the ISERROR function is to check for calculations in a worksheet that divide by zero. To see this, use TRANSFER CLEAR and then enter the value and formula specified for the following cells:

R1C1   34
R3C1   IF(ISERROR(R[−2]C/R[−1]C),"CHECK YOUR DIVISOR",
       R[−2]C/R[−1]C)

When you press ENTER, if R2C1 is blank (or contains a value of 0), Multiplan displays the message "CHECK YOUR DIVISOR" in R3C1; if a numeric value is entered in R2C1, the correct result will be entered in R3C1.

The NA Function

The NA function returns the value #N/A. The format is NA(). It is useful to place in worksheets to remind you that necessary numeric data was not available when the rest of the data was entered.

To try the NA function, first use the TRANSFER CLEAR command and then type the following values in column 1, row 1 through 4: **17, 23, NA(), 26.** (Be sure to enter the NA function with the Value command to return #N/A in that cell.) Now total the list with the following formula in R1C5:

SUM(R[−4]C:R[−1]C)

Press ENTER. The result is #N/A because there is a #N/A value in the list. If you had left R3C1 blank, the SUM function would give the result 66.

You can see that the NA function is a better indicator for cells where data is missing than is entry of a zero or blank. In the example of subtotaling coded lists, if one of the codes was not available when the data was entered, and the cell was left blank, the subtotal would be calculated with one missing value. If the NA function were entered in place of the blank, the subtotal result would be #N/A—a useful reminder that a code is missing.

The DELTA Function

The application of the DELTA function is more complex than that of many other functions. The DELTA function returns the maximum change in the absolute values of the cells from one iteration to the next. The format for DELTA is DELTA().

First use the TRANSFER CLEAR command and then consider the following example. The sales manager of a small business receives a salary of 10% on the profit of each week's sales. The company determines its net profit by subtracting the manager's salary. To do this, enter the formulas specified in the following cells:

R2C1 $15000-R[+1]C$
R3C1 $0.1*R[-1]C$
R4C1 $R[-2]C-R[-1]C$
R5C1 $DELTA()<1$

The first formula subtracts the manager's salary from the profit. The second formula calculates the salary; on the first calculation by this formula, the payment is $1500 and the message line displays, "Unresolved circular references." The third formula calculates the net profit at this stage. Finally, in R5C1, the DELTA function returns the difference between subsequent iterations. It will print TRUE if the absolute value of the difference from one iteration to the next is less than 1, and FALSE if it is not. On the first pass, however, the function returns #N/A because two values are not being compared.

Enter the Options command and change the value in the "iteration:" field to Yes and in the "completion test at:" field to R5C1. Press ENTER, and when the iteration process is completed, your screen displays the following:

```
#1      1          2       3       4       5       6       7
 1
 2   13636.35
 3    1363.635
 4   12272.715
 5      TRUE
 6
 7
```

The value in R3C1, 1363.635, represents the manager's salary. The iteration process stopped when the change in the DELTA value from one iteration to the next was less than 1. The value in R5C1, the completion test, became TRUE at this stage.

Try this same problem again, but this time change the DELTA value to less than 0.01. This time the process will proceed until the change in value from one iteration to the next is less than one cent.

Use TRANSFER CLEAR to blank your screen. Now enter the same formulas again, except in R5C1 enter DELTA()< 0.01. Again use the Options command to turn iteration on and enter R5C1 in the "completion test at:" field. Press ENTER. The values on the screen rapidly change until your screen displays the following:

```
#1      1          2       3       4       5       6       7
 1
 2   13636.364
 3    1363.6364
 4   12272.727
 5      TRUE
 6
 7
```

The NPV Function

The NPV function (NPV stands for "Net Present Value") gives you a method of analyzing an investment on the basis of your best guess of what the inflation rate will be over the lifespan of the investment.

Suppose, for example, that you can lease a building for five years for $100,000. The current renters pay $20,000 per month, and you expect the rents to increase by 12.5% per year. Is this a good investment? To see what NPV returns, use the TRANSFER CLEAR command to clear the screen and do the following. In R1C1 type the name **RENTS**, and with the Name command, apply it to R2C1 through R6C1. In R2C1 type **20000**. Move the cell pointer to R3C1 and type the formula **1.125 * R[−1]C**. Use the Copy command to copy the formula down to the next three rows. Your screen displays

```
#1         1        2        3        4        5        6        7
   1 RENTS
   2      20000
   3      22500
   4    25312.5
   5  28476.563
   6  32036.133
   7
   8
```

Place the cell pointer in R8C1 and type **NPV(0.075,RENTS)**.

Press ENTER and the value 102088.51 is returned. This value indicates that this is the amount of money you would have to place in a bank at 7.5% interest in order to receive the amount returned by the rents for the building. Since your investment was $100,000, you can consider that the lease of the building would have a greater payback than would placing the money in a bank.

Exercises

1. Try using the iteration process to add the numbers from 1 to 10. Enter the following formulas in the indicated cells:

   R1C1   RC+1
   R1C2   RC+RC[−1]
   R2C1   IF(R[−1]C=10,TRUE(),FALSE())

   With the Options command, turn on iteration and set the "completion test at:" field to R2C1. Press ENTER. You should obtain the result 55.

2. Using the data in the following illustration (repeated from "The INDEX Function" section of the chapter), apply the INDEX function to print the values contained in R5C1 and in R2C2.

#1	1	2	3	4	5	6	7
1	SCORESX						
2	23	28					
3	65	70					
4	23	28					
5	12	17					
6	90	95					
7	54	59					
8	56	61					
9	11	16					
10							
11	90						
12							
13	59						

3. Use the ideas presented in the section "Subtotaling Coded Lists" to find the sum of the medical expenses in the BUDFEB.C10 worksheet. With the Name command assign the name MEDEXP to the result.

4. Use the Xternal command to transfer the medical-expense results of Exercise 3 to the BUDSUM.C10 worksheet.

5. Find the total medical expenses in the BUDJAN.C10 and BUDMAR.C10 worksheets and transfer the results to the BUDSUM.C10 worksheet.

Using
The Math Functions

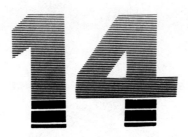

Functions

- LOG10
- LN
- EXP
- PI
- SIN
- COS
- TAN
- ATAN
- SQRT
- ABS
- SIGN
- MOD

Most of the specialized math functions in this chapter are of interest only to those in engineering or some other technical field, but some, like LOG10 and EXP, are used extensively in solving financial problems dealing with interest rates. For each of these functions, an example is given, but no mathematical formulas are derived. That is left to the mathematicians in the audience.

Using Logarithms

Multiplan has both of the standard logarithmic functions: LOG base 10 (known as common logarithms) and LN base e (known as the natural logarithm), where e = 2.7182818 . . . .

LOG10

The LOG10 function finds the common logarithm of a number. The format is LOG10(N), where N is any positive number. For example, if you type **LOG10(100)** in any cell, the value returned is 2, since 10^2 equals 100. Try another example: Type the formula **LOG10(3500)** and press ENTER. The value returned is 3.544068, since 10 raised to the power 3.544068($10^{3.544068}$) equals 3500.

LN

Now consider the natural logarithmic function, LN. The format is LN(N), where N is any positive number. The base for the natural logarithm is e, which equals 2.7182818 . . . . If you type the formula **LN(5)** in R1C1, the function returns 1.6094379, meaning that $e^{1.6094379}$ equals 5.

You can use natural logarithms to find the logarithm of a number to any base you wish. For example, the logarithm of 8 to the base 2 is 3, since 2^3 is 8. To try this, use Value and enter the following formula:

"LN2="&FIXED(LN(8)/LN(2),3)

Press ENTER and LN2 = 3.000 is displayed.

You can join two text values by using the *concatenation* operator, &. The FIXED function serves two purposes: It sets the number of digits after the decimal point to three, and it changes the result, 3.000, to a text value. When the Value command is used, any text value, in this case LN2=, must be enclosed in double quotation marks.

As mentioned at the beginning of this chapter, the logarithmic functions are useful in financial problems dealing with interest. For an example, consider the following formula:

$$Y = 1/P*LOG(A/D)/LOG(1+I/P)$$

This formula can be used to determine the time it will take for a given sum of money to increase to a certain amount at a given interest rate. It can answer the question, If you deposit $2000 in a timesaver account at 10% interest compounded daily, how long will it take before the account has reached $5000?

In the formula, let

D = DEPOSIT
A = AMOUNT you will accumulate
I = INTEREST rate
P = PERIODS per year the deposit is compounded
Y = YEARS to reach desired amount

To try this problem, clear the worksheet and enter the following headings in columns 1 through 5 of row 1: DEPOSIT, INT. RATE, PERIODS, AMOUNT, YEARS. Right-justify each of these titles and Fix the number of decimals in columns 2 and 5 at 2. In the designated cells enter

R2C1	2000
R2C2	0.1
R2C3	365
R2C4	5000
R2C5	1/RC[−2]*LOG10(RC[−1]/RC[−4])/LOG10(1+RC[−3]/RC[−2])

With the entries completed, your screen displays

```
#1        1         2        3        4        5        6        7
 1     DEPOSIT  INT. RATE  PERIODS   AMOUNT    YEARS
 2       2000      0.10       365     5000     9.16
 3
 4
 5
```

Now you'll see what effect changing the interest rate has on reaching the desired goal. In the following cells enter the following:

R3C1	R[−1]C	Copy the formula down three rows
R3C2	R[−1]C+1%	"
R3C3	R[−1]C	"
R3C4	4[−1]C	"
R3C5		Copy the formula from R2C5 down 4 rows

On completion your screen displays

```
#1        1         2        3        4        5        6        7
 1     DEPOSIT  INT. RATE  PERIODS   AMOUNT    YEARS
 2       2000      0.10       365     5000     9.16
 3       2000      0.11       365     5000     8.33
 4       2000      0.12       365     5000     7.64
 5       2000      0.13       365     5000     7.05
 6       2000      0.14       365     5000     6.55
 7
```

You can experiment with this worksheet by changing any of the variables in row 2 and see the results of those changes in column 5. Many banks compound interest quarterly; to see the effect this has, enter 4 in the PERIODS column. Note that although the LOG function was used in this formula, the LN function could be substituted without changing the results.

The EXP Function

EXP is the converse of the natural log function LN. The format is EXP(N). It raises e to the power of the argument N. For example, you just saw that LN(5)= 1.6094379; therefore, since EXP is the converse of LN, EXP(1.6094379) should be equal to 5. Try it by entering the expression in R1C1. The value returned is 4.9999999. The fractional difference is due to the natural log of 5, LN(5), being calculated to only nine significant digits. If you type **EXP(LN(5))** in R1C1 and press ENTER, the value returned is 5.

Since any number raised to the first power is equal to the number itself (for example, $10^1 = 10$, $e^1 = e$), you can see the value of e by entering on the command line

"e="&FIXED(EXP(1),5)

Press ENTER and R1C1 displays e=2.71828, the value of e calculated to five significant digits.

Now let's use the EXP function in a more practical situation. Suppose you deposit money in an IRA at your local bank. You deposit the maximum of $2000, and the bank pays 10% interest. How much will the IRA be worth in ten years? The EXP function can help you determine this with the formula

$$\text{Amount Returned} = \text{Principal} \times \text{EXP (Years} \times \text{Interest)}$$
$$= 2000 \times \text{EXP}(10*10\%)$$

In your worksheet enter

R1C2	IRA FUND	(Make R1C2:41C3 continuous)
R3C1:4	PRINCIPAL INTEREST YEARS AMOUNT	(center data)
R4C1:4	"=" (as a separator)	
R5C1	$2000	(format R5:9C1 $)
R5C2	10	(format R5:9C2:4 FIX, 2 decimals)
R5C3	10	
R5C4	RC[−3]*EXP(RC[−1]*RC[−2]%	

Press ENTER and your screen displays

```
#1        1         2         3         4        5        6        7
 1                I.R.A. FUND
 2
 3  PRINCIPAL   INTEREST    YEARS      AMOUNT
 4  ==========================================
 5  $2000.00      10.00     10.00     5436.56
 6
 7
```

Now you'll see how the amounts change at higher interest rates. Copy the data in row 5, columns 1, 3, and 4, down four rows. In R6C2 enter **11%** and increase the interest by 0.5% in each of the following rows (from 11 to 12.5%). Press ENTER and your screen now displays

```
#1        1              2           3         4          5         6          7
1                    I.R.A. FUND
2
3  PRINCIPAL    INTEREST       YEARS       AMOUNT
4  ================================================
5   $2000.00       10.00       10.00       5436.56
6   $2000.00       11.00       10.00       6008.33
7   $2000.00       11.50       10.00       6316.39
8   $2000.00       12.00       10.00       6640.23
9   $2000.00       12.50       10.00       6980.69
10
```

You can experiment with this worksheet by varying any of the values in row 5 to see how the amounts are affected.

Roots and Powers

In Chapter 13 you used a rather involved process to find an approximation of the cube root of 88. You can use the logarithmic functions to find the cube root more efficiently. The formula to use is EXP(LN(N)/R), where N stands for the number and R for the root. It will return the Rth root of the number N. To find the cube root of 88, type the formula **EXP(LN(88)/3)**. Press ENTER and the result, 4.4479602, is displayed.

You can also conveniently raise any number to a power with these functions. The formula is EXP(P*LN(N)), where N stands for the number and P for power. To calculate 6^3, type the formula **EXP(3*LN(6))**. Press ENTER and the cube of 6, 216, is displayed.

These formulas may be combined to find fractional powers of a number. For example, $16^{3/2}$ can be found with the formula EXP(3*LN(16)/2).

The PI Function

The PI function represents the mathematical constant π, which has the value 3.14159 . . . . π is a common mathematical constant that is used in many equations. For example, the formula for finding the area of a circle with a radius of 7 is $A = \pi 7^2$. Type the following formula:

PI()*7*7 or PI()*7$^\wedge$2

Press ENTER and the area of this circle, 153.93804, is displayed.

The Trigonometric Functions

Multiplan has four built-in trigonometric functions: SIN, COS, TAN, and ATAN. Like the other functions, each will return values to 14 places of accuracy if you increase the widths of the columns.

SIN

First consider the SIN function. The format is SIN(N), where the argument N is the angle measured in radians. For example, if you type the formula **SIN(PI()/2)** and press ENTER, the result returned is 1, which is the sine of an angle of $\pi/2$ radians, or 90 degrees.

If you wish to find the sine of an angle with a given measurement in degrees, the angle must be multiplied by PI()/180. For example, suppose you wish to find the sine of a 27-degree angle. Type the formula **SIN(27*PI()/180)**. Press ENTER and the sine of 27 degrees, 0.4539905, is returned.

COS

The COS function returns the cosine of an angle. The format is COS(N), where N is the measure of an angle entered in radians. Typing **COS(PI()/4)** and pressing ENTER will return the value 0.7071068.

To find the cosine of an angle expressed in degrees, multiply the angle measurement by the function PI()/180 to convert it to radians. To find the cosine of 35 degrees, for example, type the formula **COS(35∗PI()/180)**.

TAN

The TAN function returns the tangent of an angle. The format is TAN(N), where N is an angle measured in radians. Typing the formula **TAN(PI()/4)** and pressing ENTER will return the value 1.

Try developing a worksheet to produce a table for the SIN, COS, and TAN of the angles from 0 to 90 degrees in increments of 5 degrees.

In row 1, columns 1 through 4, type the following column headings: **N**, **SIN(N)**, **COS(N)**, **TAN(N)**. With the FORMAT cells command, center the entries. Also format column 1, rows 2 through 20, to center the data. In R2C1 type **0**. In R3C1 type the formula **R[−1]C+5** and copy it down to row 20; this will calculate the angle increments. Your screen now looks like Figure 14-1.

#1	1	2	3	4	5	6	7
1	N	SIN(N)	COS(N)	TAN(N)			
2	0						
3	5						
4	10						
5	15						
6	20						
7	25						
8	30						
9	35						
10	40						
11	45						
12	50						
13	55						
14	60						
15	65						
16	70						
17	75						
18	80						
19	85						
20	90						

Figure 14-1. *Worksheet with angle increments of 5 degrees entered*

#1	1	2	3	4	5	6	7
1	N	SIN(N)	COS(N)	TAN(N)			
2	0	0.0000000	1.0000000	0.0000000			
3	5	0.0871557	0.9961947	0.0874887			
4	10	0.1736482	0.9848078	0.1763270			
5	15	0.2588190	0.9659258	0.2679492			
6	20	0.3420201	0.9396926	0.3639702			
7	25	0.4226183	0.9063078	0.4663077			
8	30	0.5000000	0.8660254	0.5773503			
9	35	0.5735764	0.8191520	0.7002075			
10	40	0.6427876	0.7660444	0.8390996			
11	45	0.7071068	0.7071068	1.0000000			
12	50	0.7660444	0.6427876	1.1917536			
13	55	0.8191520	0.5735764	1.4281480			
14	60	0.8660254	0.5000000	1.7320508			
15	65	0.9063078	0.4226183	2.1445069			
16	70	0.9396926	0.3420201	2.7474774			
17	75	0.9659258	0.2588190	3.7320508			
18	80	0.9848078	0.1736482	5.6712818			
19	85	0.9961947	0.0871557	##########			
20	90	1.0000000	0.0000000	##########			

Figure 14-2.   *Worksheet with SIN, COS, and TAN formulas executed*

Enter the FORMAT cells command and in the "cells:" field enter R2C2:R20C5, in the "format code" field select Fix, and in the "# of decimals:" field type 7. Now enter the following formulas in the cells indicated:

R2C2   SIN(RC[−1]∗PI()/180)
R2C3   COS(RC[−2]∗PI()/180)
R2C4   TAN(RC[−3]∗PI()/180)

To complete the table, copy each formula down to row 20. The table should look like Figure 14-2.

ATAN

The ATAN function calculates the arctangent, or inverse tangent, of the argument. It yields the measurement of an angle expressed in radians in the range from −PI()/2 to +PI()/2. The format is ATAN(N), where N can be any number.

Entering the formula ATAN(1) in R1C1 will produce 0.785398, the measure of the angle in radians. To convert an angle in radians to degrees, multiply the formula by 180/PI(). Thus, 180/PI()*ATAN(1) produces 44.999991, the measure of the angle in degrees.

The SQRT Function

The square root function, SQRT, returns the square root of the argument. The format is SQRT(N), where N can be any positive number. If you enter the formula SQRT(456) in R1C1, the value returned is the square root of 456, 21.354157.

The ABS Function

The absolute value of a number is its positive value, regardless of whether the number is positive or negative. The ABS function returns the absolute value of the argument. The format is ABS(N), where N can be any number. If you type the formula **ABS(13.8)** and press ENTER, 13.8 is returned. If you type the formula **ABS(−13.8)** and press ENTER, the result is the same, 13.8.

The SIGN Function

The SIGN function determines if a number is positive, negative, or zero, and returns the following values accordingly:

1 if positive
0 if zero
−1 if negative

The format for the function is SIGN(N), where the argument N can be any number.

To see this function demonstrated, type the following formulas in the cells indicated:

R1C1   SIGN(34)
R2C1   SIGN(0)
R3C1   SIGN(−34)

Press ENTER and your screen display looks like this:

```
#1          1         2        3        4        5        6        7
   1             1
   2             0
   3            -1
   4
```

Use this function to graph a range of numbers. Graph positive numbers with a + symbol and negative numbers with a − symbol.

In column 1, beginning in row 1, type the following numbers: **7**, **−3**, **−8**, **6**, **1**, **0**. The numbers will be graphed in column 2. Type the following formula in R1C2:

REPT(MID("− +",SIGN(RC[−1])+2,1),ABS(RC[−1]))

Press ENTER. Copy the formula down the next five rows. Your screen should look like this:

```
#1          1         2        3        4        5        6        7
 1              7  +++++++
 2             -3  ---
 3             -8  --------
 4              6  ++++++
 5              1  +
 6              0
 7
 8
```

Now consider the formula. Recall that the format for REPT is REPT (T,Count) and for MID is MID(T,Start,Count). The arguments of the formula are illustrated here:

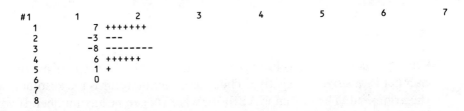

The first number, 7, is positive, so the function SIGN(RC[−1] returns a value of 1. This value is then added to 2, telling Multiplan to start at the third character of MID's text value − + (note the space between − and +). In this way the + sign is selected for graphing a positive number. The function SIGN will return −1 in rows 2 and 3, and 0 in row 6. The final MID argument, Count, is 1, which means "take one character." The final argument of the REPT function, ABS(RC[−1]), tells Multiplan to print the character seven times. The value returned by this argument will always be positive because of the ABS function.

The MOD Function

The MOD function is used to return the remainder when one number is divided by another. The number returned has the same sign as the divisor. The format for MOD is MOD(Dividend, Divisor). For example, if you type the formula **MOD(17,5)** and press ENTER, the value returned is 2, since 17 divided by 5 equals

3 with a remainder of 2. The MOD function returns only the remainder.

The algorithm that Multiplan uses to find the value returned by the MOD function is

$$MOD(X,Y)=X-INT(X/Y)*Y$$

Typing the formula **MOD(−17,−5)** and pressing ENTER produces the result −2, but typing **MOD(−17,5)** and pressing ENTER produces a value of 3. To see why, substitute the values into the formula to work through the division:

$$
\begin{aligned}
MOD(-17,5) &= -17-INT(-17/5)*5 \\
&= -17-INT(-3.4)*5 \\
&= -17-(-4)*5 \\
&= -17+20 \\
&= 3
\end{aligned}
$$

$$
\begin{aligned}
MOD(-17,-5) &= -17-INT(-17/(-5))*(-5) \\
&= -17-INT(3.4)*(-5) \\
&= -17-(3)*(-5) \\
&= -17+15 \\
&= -2
\end{aligned}
$$

The formula MOD(17,−5) returns −3. You can verify the result by substituting the arguments in the formula.

Exercises

1. a. Use the LN and EXP functions to find the cube roots of 64 and 125.
   b. Use the same functions to find 2 raised to the l0th power.

2. Use the PI function to find the area of a circle with a diameter of 5 1/4 inches (your disk).

3. Find the SIN, COS, and TAN of 135 degrees.

4. Modify the following formula (used in the chapter) to graph the following data: 133, −125, −99, 117, 106, −97.

```
REPT(MID("- +",SIGN(RC[-1])+2,1),ABS(RC[-1]))
```

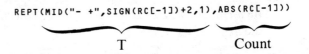

T   Count

Appendix A
Key Summary

The following table lists the key or keys used to perform various Multiplan operations. The column titled IBM Key identifies the keys used on the IBM PC (PC DOS version 1.1) and its look-alikes. The column titled Non-IBM Code gives the generic codes used by Microsoft for the CP/M-80 version of Multiplan. The last column, Your Computer, is left blank so you can fill in the appropriate codes for your system. If your computer has more or fewer function keys than the IBM, or if they perform different functions, you should fill in the proper values in the column. In the following table, the symbol $^\wedge$ represents the CONTROL key, usually labeled CTRL on the keyboard.

Function	Description	IBM Key	Non-IBM Code	Your Computer
UP	Moves the cell pointer up one cell.	↑	$^\wedge$E	
DOWN	Moves the cell pointer down one cell.	↓	$^\wedge$X	
LEFT	Moves the cell pointer left one cell.	←	$^\wedge$S	
RIGHT	Moves the cell pointer right one cell.	→	$^\wedge$D	
PAGE UP	Moves the screen up to display the 20 rows above the current display.	PgUp	$^\wedge$R$^\wedge$E	
PAGE DOWN	Moves the screen down to display the 20 rows below the current display.	PgDn	$^\wedge$R$^\wedge$X	
PAGE LEFT	Displays the next page to the left of the current screen display. When the column widths are in the default setting (10 characters), the screen displays 7 columns to the left.	$^\wedge$←	$^\wedge$R$^\wedge$S	
PAGE RIGHT	Displays the next page to the right of the current screen display. If columns are in the default setting, the screen displays the next 7 columns.	$^\wedge$→	$^\wedge$R$^\wedge$D	
HOME	Moves the cell pointer to the upper-left corner of the display.	Home	$^\wedge$Q	

Function	Description	IBM Key	Non-IBM Code	Your Computer
END	Moves the cell pointer to the right of the last cell on the screen that contains data or to the right of the last formatted cell.	End	$^\wedge$Z	
NEXT WINDOW	Moves the cell pointer to the next window. When the last window is reached, pressing F1 moves the cell pointer to the first window.	F1	$^\wedge$W	
NEXT UNLOCKED CELL	Moves the cell pointer to the next unlocked cell that is not blank.	F2	$^\wedge$F	
CANCEL	Cancels the current command and returns the screen to the main command menu.	Esc	$^\wedge$C	
RETURN	Executes the command you selected from the command line.	↵	ENTER	
NEXT COMMAND	Moves the edit cursor to the next command in the command line.	← →	$^\wedge$I	
PREVIOUS COMMAND	Moves the edit cursor to the previous command in the command line.	←	$^\wedge$H	
FORWARD TAB	Moves to, and selects the contents of, the next field in the command line.	← →	$^\wedge$I	
HELP	Displays information about the command highlighted in the command line or about the command in progress.	Alt H	?	
RECALCULATE	Recalculates the entire worksheet. If the command is pressed when a formula is displayed, the formula is replaced by its result.	F4	!	
DELETE	Deletes the character or characters under the edit cursor in entries you have made.	Del	$^\wedge$Y	
CHARACTER RIGHT	Moves the edit cursor to the next character to the right. If the command line is displayed, moves the cursor one command to the right.	F10	$^\wedge$L	
CHARACTER LEFT	Moves the edit cursor to the next character to the left. If the command line is displayed, moves the cursor one command to the left.	F9	$^\wedge$K	
WORD RIGHT	When a command is selected, moves the edit cursor to the next word to the right.	F8	$^\wedge$P	

Function	Description	IBM Key	Non-IBM Code	Your Computer
WORD LEFT	When a command is selected, moves the edit cursor to the next word to the left.	F7	^O	
REFERENCE	Changes relative reference to absolute reference.	F3	@	
to R1C1	Moves the cell pointer to R1C1 from any location in the worksheet.	^PgUp	^Q	

Appendix B
Commands

The following general comments apply to Multiplan's commands.

Selecting Commands and Subcommands

Commands may be selected by (1) pressing ENTER when the edit cursor highlights the command, or (2) pressing the first letter of the command. Both methods may also be used to select subcommands.

Default Field Entries

For most commands, the default values entered in the various fields are determined by the position of the cell pointer when the command is entered. In command fields that list more than one choice, the choice currently in force is enclosed by parentheses. To change the setting from a default value, use the TAB key to move the edit cursor to that field and use the space bar or character keys to make the selection.

Exiting Commands

To exit a command without having it carried out, press ESC. This will also return you to the main command menu.

Executing Commands

Commands are carried out by pressing ENTER.

The Commands

ALPHA:
> Places text in the active cell. Complete the command by pressing ENTER or one of the arrow keys that move the cell pointer.

BLANK cells: R3C3
> Replaces the contents of the active cell with spaces. Groups of cells may be blanked by use of the range operator or of Name references.

COPY Right Down From
> Offers three ways of copying cells into other cells.

> > COPY RIGHT number of cells:___   starting at:
> > Copies a single cell or column of cells to the right.

> > COPY DOWN number of cells: starting at:
> > Copies a cell or group of cells down the number of rows you specify.

> > COPY FROM cells: to cells:
> > Copies a single cell or group of cells to another section of the worksheet. If a group of cells is copied and the designation is to a single cell, that cell is considered the upper-left corner of the group.

DELETE: Row Column
> Offers the choice of deleting either complete or partial rows and columns. The remaining portion of the active worksheet adjusts to fill the deleted section.

> > DELETE ROW # of rows: starting at:
> >   between columns: and:
> > Allows you to delete complete or partial rows. The default values are displayed in the fields.

> > DELETE COLUMN # of columns: starting at:
> >   between rows: and:
> > Allows you to delete complete or partial columns. The default values are displayed in the fields.

EDIT:
> Used to edit text, formulas, or data in the active cell. If while in the Edit command you press one of the keys that move the cell pointer instead of

ENTER, data is entered in the active cell and you remain in the Edit command.

EXTERNAL: Copy List Use:
Offers a choice of three subcommands to be used with Xternal worksheets.

EXTERNAL COPY from sheet: name:
                               to: linked:(Yes)No
Allows you to extract data from a worksheet that resides on a disk and to transfer that data to the active worksheet.

EXTERNAL LIST:
Displays the names of the worksheets supporting the active worksheet and also of those depending on the active worksheet.

EXTERNAL USE filename: instead of:
Allows you to substitute another worksheet for a previously assigned supporting worksheet. The substitute worksheet must have a format identical to the supporting worksheet.

FORMAT: Cells Default Options Width
Offers a variety of ways to format the entire worksheet or sections of it. Allows you to control the alignment and format code of the contents of each cell. The alignment and format code options, along with their meanings, are as follows:

Alignment Options

Def	Default	Alignment is set by the Format Cells command.
Ctr	Center	Centers the cell's contents in the column.
Gen	General	Aligns text left and numbers right.
Left	Left	Left-justifies the contents of the cell in the column.
Right	Right	Right-justifies the contents of the cell in the column.
—		Allows you to change format code without changing alignment code.

Format Codes

Def	Default	Formats the contents of the cell as set by the Format Default command.
Cont	Continuous	Allows cell contents to carry over into succeeding cells provided they are blank.
Exp	Exponent	Displays numbers in scientific notation (that is, a decimal times a power of 10).
Fix	Fix Decimal	Displays numbers rounded to the number of decimal places you set in the "# of decimals:" field.
Gen	General	Displays numbers as accurately as possible in the column width provided.
Int	Integer	Rounds numbers to the nearest integer.
$	Dollar	Displays numbers in standard dollar notation ($ sign and two decimal places).
*	Bar graph	Displays a bar to represent the number in the cell. Decimal numbers are rounded to the nearest integer.
%	Percent	Displays numbers as percents. The number of decimals is set in the "# of decimals:" field.
—		Allows you to change alignment without changing format code.

FORMAT cells: alignment:(Def)Ctr Gen Left Right —
format code:(Def)Cont Exp Fix Gen Int $ * % — # of decimals: 0
Allows you to alter the alignment and format of the contents of one or more cells.

FORMAT DEFAULT: Cells Width
Enables you to choose settings other than default values for the entire worksheet.

FORMAT DEFAULT CELLS alignment: Ctr(Gen)Left Right
format code: Cont Exp Fix(Gen)Int $ * % # of decimals: 0
The options in each of these fields, alignment and format code, are the same as the one just given. Choices made here affect the entire worksheet, rather than individual cells or groups of cells.

FORMAT DEFAULT width in chars:___
> Changes the width of all columns that have the default value of 10.

FORMAT OPTIONS commas: Yes (No)   formulas: Yes (No)
> The commas option separates numbers into groups of 1000 and places a comma between the groups. The formula option is used to display formulas on the worksheet, rather than the formulas' results.

FORMAT WIDTH in chars or d(efault):d   column: through:
> Alters the width of a column or continuous group of columns to the value you set. The maximum width of columns is 32 characters.

GOTO: Name Row-col Window
> Enables you to go directly to a specific section of the worksheet.

> GOTO name:
>> Moves the cell pointer directly to the upper-left corner of the group of cells designated by the name you supply.

> GOTO row: column:
>> Moves the cell pointer directly to the cell that you specify in the row and column fields.

> GOTO WINDOW window number: row: column:
>> Moves the cell pointer to the window you designate and places the cell designated by the row and column numbers in the home position.

HELP: Resume Start Next Previous Application Commands Editing Formulas Keyboard
> Loads the Help file from your disk into the computer. You may then select from the menu the Multiplan operation for which you want to receive help. Pressing ESC returns you to the main command menu.

> HELP Resume
>> Returns you to the same point you were when you entered the Help command.

> HELP Start
>> Moves the screen display to the beginning of the Help file.

> HELP Next
>> Moves to the next screen display of the Help file.

> HELP Previous
>> Moves to the previous screen display of the Help file.

HELP Application
Displays a list of common Multiplan difficulties and gives the names of the commands that will help remedy them.

HELP Commands
Displays text explaining the various Multiplan commands, starting with the Alpha command.

HELP Editing
Displays the section of the Help file explaining Multiplan's editing features.

HELP Formulas
Displays the section of the Help file related to formulas.

HELP Keyboard
Displays the section of the Help file that explains the special keys used for performing specific Multiplan functions.

INSERT: Row Column
Allows you to insert complete or partial rows or columns into the Multiplan worksheet.

INSERT ROW # of rows: 1   before row:
between columns: 1   and: 63

Allows you to designate a row or portion of a row and where it is to be inserted.

INSERT COLUMN # of columns: 1   before column:
between rows: 1   and: 255

Allows you to designate a column or portion of a column and where it is to be inserted.

LOCK: Cells Formulas
Gives you two ways of locking the contents of cells so they may not be changed accidentally.

LOCK cells:—   status: Locked (Unlocked)
Allows you to change the status, locked or unlocked, of the section of the worksheet you designate in the cells field.

LOCK formulas:
Enter Y in this field to lock all cells containing formulas or text.

MOVE Row Column
>   Allows you to move whole rows or whole columns only.

>> MOVE ROW from row: 1   to before row: 1   # of rows: 1
>>   You designate the row or rows you wish to move and their destination.

>> MOVE COLUMN   from column: 1   to left of column: 1
>>   # of columns: 1
>>   You designate the column or columns you wish to move and their destination.

NAME: define name: to refer to:
>   Allows you to designate a name to apply to a cell or group of cells.

OPTIONS recalc: Yes No   mute Yes(No)
>   iteration: Yes(No)   completion test at:
>   Allows you to:

> 1. Turn off recalculation so that the sheet recalculates only when you press F4.
> 2. Mute (turn off) the bell so that it does not beep when an error is made.
> 3. Turn on the iteration process.

PRINT: Printer File Margins Options
>   Sends output to the printer or a disk and controls output format.

>> PRINT on printer:
>>   Starts printing the active worksheet immediately. The default values of the margins and option choices will be used unless you change them before selecting the Printer subcommand.

>> PRINT on file:
>>   Prints your worksheet on the disk instead of at the printer. You must enter a filename before the worksheet will be printed on the disk. Again, the default values of margins and option choices will be used unless you change them before selecting this command.

>> PRINT MARGINS: left: 5   top: 6   print width: 70
>>   print length: 54   page length: 66
>>   Controls the positioning of the printout on paper. The default values displayed are for standard 8 1/2- by 11-inch paper. They may be changed if a nonstandard-sized paper is used.

PRINT OPTIONS: area: setup:
      formulas: Yes(No)   row-col numbers: Yes(No)
Allows you to print a specific area of your worksheet and to control certain printer functions. You can choose to print formulas or their results or row and column numbers.

QUIT:
Allows you to leave Multiplan and return to your disk operating system. You are asked to confirm this option by entering a Y for yes. If you have not saved your worksheet prior to selecting the Quit command, it will be lost when you return to the operating system.

SORT by column: between rows: and: order:($>$)$<$
Allows you to sort the contents of a designated column in either ascending or descending order. Both numeric and text values may be sorted.

TRANSFER: Load Save Clear Delete Options Rename
Offers six options that apply to the entire worksheet.

TRANSFER LOAD filename:__
Allows you to move a worksheet from the disk to the computer. Before making any entries in the filename field, you can display the directory of the logged-in disk by pressing an arrow key.

TRANSFER SAVE filename:
Saves your active worksheet on disk. The default name is supplied in the filename field. This may be changed if you wish.

TRANSFER CLEAR filename:
Clears the active worksheet. You are asked to confirm this choice by entering a Y for yes. Once cleared, your worksheet will no longer be available; the command resets the format and alignment codes to default values.

TRANSFER DELETE filename:
Deletes a file from the disk. You may enter the filename in the field or you may use the arrow keys to select the filename from the disk directory.

TRANSFER OPTIONS mode: Normal Symbolic Other setup:
This command offers several choices:

Normal: Normal mode, the standard method of saving a Multiplan worksheet.

Symbolic: Designed primarily for use by programmers. It allows you to transfer a Multiplan worksheet into a program you have written, or information from your program into a Multiplan worksheet.

Other: Used primarily for loading VisiCalc files. You cannot save a program in this mode.

Setup: Allows you to change the logged drive so you can display the directory on a second drive.

TRANSFER RENAME filename:
Allows you to rename the active worksheet and adjust the external links to supporting and dependent worksheets.

VALUE:
Used to enter numeric values or formulas. The Value command may be selected in several ways:

1. Pressing ENTER with the Value command highlighted.
2. Pressing **V**.
3. Pressing any of the digits 0-9.
4. Typing one of the characters $= + -.($". If one of these characters (except for the equals sign) is pressed, it becomes the first character of the formula.

WINDOW: Split Border Close Link Paint
Entering the Window command presents these choices:

WINDOW SPLIT: Horizontal Vertical Titles
When you select the Window Split subcommand, you are offered a choice of additional subcommands.

WINDOW SPLIT HORIZONTAL at row:
linked: Yes(No)
Allows you to split the screen horizontally into two windows at the row you enter in the row field.

WINDOW SPLIT VERTICAL at column: 9
linked: Yes(No)
Allows you to split the screen vertically into two windows at the column you enter in the column field.

WINDOW SPLIT TITLES: # of rows: 3
# of columns: 0
Splits the screen into either two or four windows.
When this command is invoked, the windows are
automatically linked and cannot be unlinked.

WINDOW change border in window number:
Used to add or delete a border. If the window has a border, it
is deleted. If it does not have a border, the border is added.

WINDOW CLOSE window number:
Loses the window that you designate in the window number
field.

WINDOW LINK window number: with window number:
linked: Yes(No)
Used to change the links between windows. Only a window
that shares the split relationship may be linked. If window #2
is split from window #1 and window #3 split from window
#2, then window #3 may be linked to window #2 but not to
window #1.

WINDOW PAINT foreground: background: border:
For use with color monitors. You can select separate colors
for the characters, background, and border of the worksheet.

Appendix C

Functions and Arguments

This appendix lists all functions available in Multiplan and arguments used by functions, along with their meanings.

Function	Remarks
ABS(N)	Returns the absolute value of the argument N.
AND(List)	Returns TRUE if all the arguments you specify in the list are true. Returns FALSE if any argument in the list is false.
ATAN(N)	Returns the arctangent of the argument. The value returned is a measurement of an angle expressed in radians in the range $-PI/2$ to $+PI/2$.
AVERAGE(List)	Returns the average of the numbers you specify in the list.
COLUMN()	Returns the number of the column in which the formula containing the function appears.
COS(N)	Returns the cosine of the argument. The angle must be entered in radians.
COUNT(List)	Returns the count of the number of items in the list that are numeric values.
DELTA()	Used to determine the change in a cell or portion of the worksheet from one iteration to the next. On the first pass through the worksheet the value returned will be #N/A.
DOLLAR(N)	Converts the argument to text in $ format. If the number is negative, the display is shown in parentheses.

Function	Remarks
EXP(N)	Calculates e(2.71828 . . .), the base of the natural logarithm to the power of the argument. EXP is the inverse of the LN function.
FALSE()	Returns the logical value FALSE.
FIXED(N,Digits)	Converts the argument N to text with the number of decimal places determined by the Digits argument.
IF(Logical, Then Value, Else Value)	Returns the Then Value if the logical value is TRUE. Returns the Else Value if the logical value is FALSE. The values returned may be numeric, text, or logical.
INDEX(Area, Subscripts)	Returns the value of a cell you select by subscripts. If one row or column represents the area, a single subscript is used. If a rectangular block is used for the area, two subscripts are required.
INT(N)	Returns the largest integer that is less than or equal to the argument, truncating any fraction instead of rounding it into integer form.
ISERROR(Value)	Returns the logical value TRUE if any of Multiplan's error values are returned. See Appendix D for error values.
ISNA(Value)	Returns the logical value TRUE only if the #N/A error is returned.
ITERCNT()	Counts the number of passes through the iteration process.
LEN(T)	Returns the number of characters in a text value. Counts spaces and all punctuation marks as well as letters and numbers.
LN(N)	Returns the natural logarithm of the argument. The argument must be a positive number.
LOG10(N)	Returns the common logarithm of a number. The argument must be a positive number.

Function	Remarks
LOOKUP(N,Table)	Searches for the number N in the first row or column of the table and returns the number from the last row or column of the table. If the table is square or higher than it is wide, LOOKUP searches the first column and returns the value from the last column of the same row. If the table is wider than it is high, LOOKUP searches the first row and returns the value from the last row of the same column.
MAX(List)	Searches a list of numbers and returns the largest value from the list.
MID(T,Start,Count)	Returns the characters you specify from the text value T. Start specifies where the first character is to be selected, and Count specifies the number of characters to be taken from that position.
MIN(List)	Searches the list you specify and returns the smallest value. Any blank cells in the list are ignored.
MOD(Dividend, Divisor)	Returns the remainder when the number you specify as the dividend is divided by the number you specify as the divisor. If the divisor is negative, the remainder will be negative.
NA()	Returns the symbol #N/A when this function is entered in a cell. Use the function to indicate cells in which you will later enter data.
NOT(Logical)	Changes the logical TRUE value to FALSE and the logical FALSE value to TRUE.
NPV(Rate,List)	Given some particular interest rate, this function calculates the amount of money you need now to produce a specific cash flow in the future.
OR(List)	Returns TRUE if any value in the list you specify is true; otherwise, returns FALSE.
PI()	Returns the approximate mathematical constant pi, 3.14159 . . . . Multiplan provides this constant to 14 places.

Function	Remarks
REPT(T,Count)	Returns the text value you specify in T the number of times you specify in Count.
ROUND(N,Digits)	Returns the number N rounded to the number of digits you specify by the argument Digits.
ROW()	Returns the number of the row in which the formula containing the function appears.
SIGN(N)	Returns 1 if the argument is positive, 0 if the argument is 0, and −1 if the argument is negative.
SIN(N)	Returns the sine of the argument. The angle must be entered in radians.
SQRT(N)	Calculates the square root of the argument. The argument must be a positive number.
STDEV(List)	Returns the standard deviation for the numbers in the list.
SUM(List)	Calculates and returns the sum of the numbers in the list.
TAN(N)	Returns the tangent of the angle. The angle must be expressed in radians.
TRUE()	Returns the logical value TRUE.
VALUE(T)	The argument for VALUE must be the text form of a number. Returned is the numeric value of that text. Arguments entered in parentheses will be returned as negative numeric values.

Argument	**Meaning**
Area	Represents a block or group of cells.
Count	Determines the number of characters to print from the starting position in a text value.
Digits	Represents the number of digits to follow a decimal point.
List	Represents a list of numbers. They may be entered individually or by Name, absolute, or relative reference.
Logical	Represents a logical expression.
N	Represents a single number or a formula that produces a single number.
Rate	Represents interest rate.
Start	Represents the starting position of a text value.
Subscripts	Designates an individual cell within a block or group of cells.
T	Represents text. The text may be entered directly or by a formula that produces text.
Table	Represents a portion of a row or column or a rectangular group of cells.
Value	May represent the logical value TRUE or FALSE, or numeric or text values, depending on the function.

Appendix D
Error Values

If you incorrectly enter a Multiplan command, function, or reference, an error value will result. The origin of the error may not be in the cell that displays the error. For example, suppose R1C1 equals 5 and R1C2 equals 0; if in R1C3 you enter the formula R1C1/R1C2, R1C3 will display the error value #DIV/0!. The source of the error is R1C2. In complicated formulas you may have to examine several cells to find the source of the error. Multiplan's error values are as follows:

Error Value   **Meaning**

#DIV/0   You have attempted to divide by 0.

#NAME?   You have made reference to a name that is undefined.

#N/A   You have made reference to a value that is not available. Keep in mind that a blank cell does not necessarily produce a "not available" error value. For example, if you add numbers in a column that contains a blank cell, the result will be the sum of the numbers present; the blank cell will be ignored. Note also that using the NA function may produce this reference.

#NULL!   You have specified an intersection of groups of cells that have no intersection.

#NUM!   A number has overflowed the limits of Multiplan's calculation. It is either too large or too small (in the latter case, having too many zeros to the right of the decimal), or you have asked Multiplan to perform an illegal operation such as SQRT(−1).

Error Value	Meaning

#REF!   You have made a reference to a deleted cell or, less commonly, to a cell outside the Multiplan worksheet, that is, beyond column 63 or below row 255.

#VALUE!   There are three possibilities here: (a) text is used when Multiplan needs a value; (b) a value is referred to when Multiplan needs text; (c) a reference is used when Multiplan needs a value.

Appendix E
Operators

Multiplan supports the following mathematical operators:

+	Add	−	Subtract
/	Divide	*	Multiply
^	Exponentiation	%	Percent

Multiplan returns the logical value TRUE or FALSE when two numbers are compared by use of relational operators:

<	less than	<=	less than or equal
=	equal	>=	greater than or equal
>	greater than	<>	not equal

The ampersand (&) is used by Multiplan to perform concatenation:

Text operator
&

INDEX